FROZEN TOMBS

FROZEN TOMBS

THE CULTURE AND ART OF
THE ANCIENT TRIBES OF SIBERIA

Published for
The Trustees of the British Museum by
British Museum Publications Limited

© 1978, The Trustees of the British Museum
ISBN 0 7141 0096 X *cased*
ISBN 0 7141 0097 8 *paper*
Published by British Museum Publications Ltd
6 Bedford Square, London WC1B 3RA

Photography by V. Terebenin
Designed by Harry Green
Set in Monotype Bembo by
Filmtype Services Ltd., Scarborough
Printed in Great Britain by
Balding and Mansell Ltd., London and Wisbech

CONTENTS

COLOUR PLATES
pages 33–40

PREFACE

Frozen Tombs is the latest of a series of exhibitions in which the State Hermitage Museum, Leningrad, is co-operating with the British Museum. On this occasion the British Museum is delighted to have the opportunity of bringing to Britain a remarkable exhibition which it is hoped will appeal to a variety of tastes, comprising as it does items of archaeological, aesthetic and historical interest. These include, as well as a magnificent series of gold ornaments from the Siberian Collection of Peter the Great, a selection of exceptionally well-preserved organic objects – leather, fabric and wood – some belonging to a people who lived 400 or 500 years before the birth of Christ. Material of this type and age rarely survives in northern latitudes except in unusual environmental conditions and the British Museum is therefore pleased that its new exhibition gallery is to be inaugurated with such a fascinating, if at times macabre, display.

The Trustees of the British Museum wish to express their thanks to Mr I. V. Popov, Deputy Minister of Culture of the Soviet Union, the State Hermitage Museum, Leningrad and in particular to its Director, Professor B. B. Piotrovsky, for their generosity in lending this material and they look forward to further fruitful co-operation. The Trustees would also like to thank Dr I. M. Stead of the Department of Prehistoric & Romano-British Antiquities and Mr G. B. Morris, Secretary of the British Museum, for his invaluable assistance in translating this catalogue.

D. M. WILSON
Director of the British Museum

FOREWORD

Among the rich archaeological treasures in the State Hermitage Museum, Leningrad, the collection of antiquities from Siberia, in particular those from the excavations of barrows of the sixth to fourth centuries BC in the High Altai, occupy a special place. They supplement the world-famous collection of gold artefacts from the Scythian barrows north of the Black Sea with objects which do not usually survive from ancient times – textiles, wood carvings, and articles of leather – preserved in the barrows of the High Altai because of the permanently frozen ground which formed under the stone cairns. Excavations between 1929 and 1954 brought to light a new world which links the eastern regions of nomadic culture with the west and reveals a remarkable uniformity of culture over the vast expanse of the Eurasian steppes.

The finds from the Altai and from other areas of Siberia show connections not only with the world of the Scythians but also with Persia and the Far East – connections which are illustrated in this exhibition by Achaemenid textiles from Persia and silk fabric from China. The exhibition also contains fascinating objects of gold from the so-called 'Siberian Collection of Peter the Great', excavated at the beginning of the eighteenth century and preserved in museums for 250 years.

The Hermitage and the British Museum in recent years have established a good working relationship and a useful exchange of interesting exhibitions. I hope that this exhibition, which will give visitors to the British Museum their first opportunity to familiarise themselves with the ancient culture of Siberia, will also arouse great interest and serve the cause of further fruitful contacts between the museums of the Soviet Union and Great Britain.

BORIS PIOTROVSKY
Director of the Hermitage

EURASIA

Showing the Location of Southern Siberia and Neighbouring Regions

SIBERIA

URAL MOUNTAINS

• Leningrad

• Moscow

SOUTHERN SIBERIA

MANCHURIA

KAMCHATKA

CARPATHIAN Mts.

SCYTHIA

KAZAKHSTAN

MONGOLIA

Danube

BLACK SEA

CASPIAN SEA

Volga

Dnepr

Great Wall

Oxus

MEDITERRANEAN

Euphrates

PERSIA

TIBET

Hwang Ho

CHINA

Yenisei

Ob

Irtysh

0   1000   2000 Km.

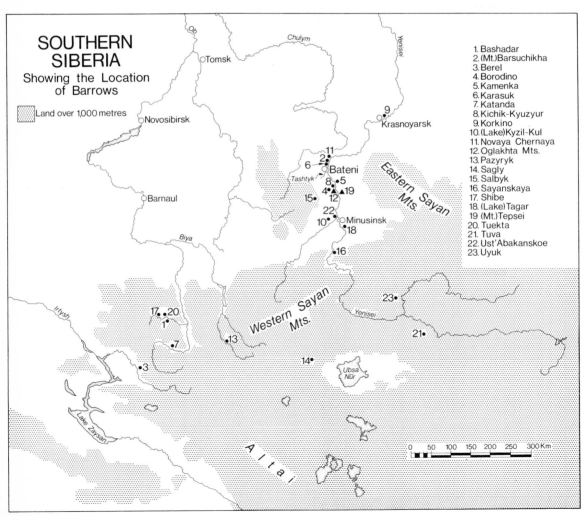

SOUTHERN SIBERIA

Showing the Location of Barrows

Land over 1,000 metres

1. Bashadar
2. (Mt.)Barsuchikha
3. Berel
4. Borodino
5. Kamenka
6. Karasuk
7. Katanda
8. Kichik-Kyuzyur
9. Korkino
10. (Lake)Kyzil-Kul
11. Novaya Chernaya
12. Oglakhta Mts.
13. Pazyryk
14. Sagly
15. Salbyk
16. Sayanskaya
17. Shibe
18. (Lake)Tagar
19. (Mt.)Tepsei
20. Tuekta
21. Tuva
22. Ust'Abakanskoe
23. Uyuk

Ob

Chulym

○ Tomsk

Yenisei

○ Novosibirsk

9 •○ Krasnoyarsk

11 •

2 •

6 ○ • Bateni

Tashtyk

8 ○• • 5

4 •▲ ▲ 19

12

15 •

22

○ Barnaul

Biya

10 • ○ Minusinsk

• 18

Eastern Sayan Mts.

• 16

23 •

Western Sayan Mts.

Yenisei

21 •

Irtysh

17 • • 20
    1 •

• 7

• 13

14 •

Ubsa Nür

• 3

Lake Zaysan

A l t a i

0 50 100 150 200 250 300 Km

INTRODUCTION

The seven thousand kilometres from the foothills of the Carpathians to Mongolia is spanned by a great belt of steppes, bounded on the north by forests and on the south by seas, mountains and deserts. In these vast and abundant grasslands numerous flocks of sheep and herds of horses and cattle could be maintained the whole year round, and it was here, from the seventh to the third centuries BC that a community of pastoral peoples gradually took shape. In the history of the ancient nomadic tribes this period was marked by constant migrations, conflicts over pastures, and wars to seize cattle and booty. It saw the rise of mounted war-bands armed with swords, bows and arrows, and lances, and of military alliances. With the acquisition of wealth a tribal and military aristocracy developed.

Scholars have given the conventional title 'Scythian' to these peoples, using the proper name of a powerful union of tribes which was based on the steppes north of the Black Sea, and created one of its most striking cultures. The nomadic groups which ruled the Eurasian steppes for more than five centuries were linked by their North-Iranian languages, by European-type physical character-istics and perhaps also by a common origin. There was a certain unity of culture and art because of their shared level of social development as well as political and trading contacts, but each group retained individual features. The question of their origins and ethnic history is complicated and disputed, but there is no argument about the significance of their artistic achievements which have now become an established part of world culture.

From the varied culture of the vast Scythian world we present here the culture of the tribes of Southern Siberia, an area which includes the Altai, Tuva, the Minusinsk basin and the basin of the Middle Yenisei, together with part of the magnificent but unprovenanced Siberian Collection of Peter the Great.

Little is known about the creators of the culture and art of the Southern Siberian tribes. They possessed neither writing nor coinage, and were far away from the ancient literate civilizations whose historians knew of them only as legendary tribes. The Scythians and their way of life were described by the Greek historian Herodotus, who visited the lands north of the Black Sea in the fifth century BC, but the further east from Scythia the more mysterious were the inhabitants. Some scholars identify the Altai tribes with the 'gold-guarding gryphons' of Herodotus, whilst others include them in the Yue-chi tribes and call the inhabitants of the Minusinsk basin 'Din-Lin'. These statements however,

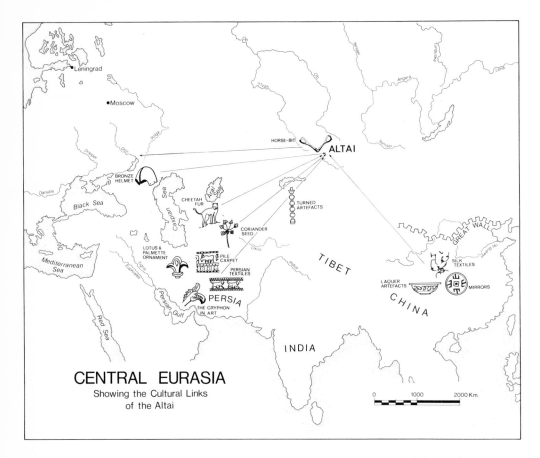

CENTRAL EURASIA
Showing the Cultural Links
of the Altai

taken from the later Chinese dynastic chronicles, are as unreliable as the reports of Herodotus. Many Soviet scholars refer to the Siberian contemporaries of the Scythians simply as Early Nomads.

The emerging unity of these peoples is most strikingly expressed in their art – the so-called Scytho-Siberian 'Animal Style'. Its origins are still obscure, but one of several interpretations – the 'Asiatic theory' – has a particular relevance for the present exhibition. Late Bronze Age artefacts, Karasuk knives and daggers decorated with the heads of goats, rams and elk, have been found in the Minusinsk basin. In this same area the earliest fully-developed examples of the animal style (eighth and early seventh centuries BC) were found in Tuva, near the village of Uyuk, during the excavation of the royal barrow of Arzhan in 1971. The art of the Arzhan finds is naturalistic, but it contains the foundations of the techniques of stylization which are the essence of the animal style. The proponents of the 'Asiatic theory', who have multiplied since the 1971 discoveries, regard the art of the Karasuk bronzes as the precursor of the animal style, and the Arzhan finds as the earliest known objects in the Scytho-Siberian style. However, we must not anticipate events and time, and possibly new discoveries, will elucidate this problem.

THE SIBERIAN COLLECTION OF PETER THE GREAT

Catalogue numbers 1–10

The Siberian Collection of Peter the Great is one of the most remarkable of ancient collections. Formed 250 years ago, it has not yet been fully studied and many of the problems related to it still await solution.

The age of Peter the Great was responsible for rapid development in industry and advances in all spheres of knowledge, including the natural and historical sciences. It was Peter the Great's aim to establish the history of his country and so interest was aroused in the ancient cultures of Russia, resulting in the collecting of gold antiquities and works of art. In January 1716, according to the documentary evidence, the first ten gold antiquities were delivered to the Tsar's court by the Governor of Siberia, M. P. Gagarin (cat. nos. 3 and 7). It was about this time that Peter the Great, who appreciated the scholarly and artistic significance of such objects, issued Edicts, Instructions and oral commands to ensure that they were collected at the expense of the State Treasury. Although these early Edicts have not been found, their existence is attested by references in the letters of Governors and official functionaries who sent antiquities and other 'curiosities' to the Court. Peter's surviving Edicts and Instructions, which relate to 1718, required that unusual antiquities should be collected and drawings made of whatever was found. Considerable attention was paid to inscribed objects in order to identify the people who had made and used them, and a special Edict prohibited the concealing and melting down of antiquities. These efforts resulted between 1716 and 1718, in the Tsar receiving from Tobolsk, capital of the Province of Siberia, some two hundred ancient gold and silver articles acquired by the Chancellery of the Governor, M. P. Gagarin. These pieces had probably been obtained from the 'mound-men' who also operated in the steppe beyond the frontiers of Siberia carrying on their trade of 'excavating' ancient barrows.

The consignments from Tobolsk, accompanied by inventories showing the number and weight of the objects, were first examined by the Tsar and then added to other acquisitions to form a collection which became a national treasure of both artistic and scholarly interest. In 1727 it was transferred to the first public museum in Russia, the *Kunstkammer*, where it was put on exhibition. Then, in 1859, through the good offices of S. G. Stroganov, President of the newly founded Imperial Archaeological Commission, it passed to the Hermitage where the rest of the collection was added in 1894.

As early as the eighteenth century the collection had become an enigma, not least because the local archives had been destroyed in a fire at Tobolsk in 1788. However, at the end of the nineteenth century the famous Russian archaeologist, A. A. Spitsyn, discovered in Peter the Great's archives a series of letters and inventories which had accompanied consignments of antiquities from the Province of Siberia. This led Spitsyn to call the collection 'Siberian', and that description has now become firmly established. Soviet archaeologists have named the collection in honour of Peter the Great in recognition of the strict measures of conservation which led to the preservation of these unique antiquities.

In the *Kunstkammer* objects of gold from other sources were added, but comparative examination of the Siberian Collection has established that the bulk of it was sent from Tobolsk. The source of the rest has yet to be determined, and the precise provenances of the objects from the entire collection are as obscure as the nature of the monuments from which they came. From indirect evidence it is clear that the territory in question was to the west of the Altai, within the boundless steppes of Kazakhstan, and probably belonged to a group of Sakic tribes. Viewed from a Scythian standpoint it is the very centre of the nomadic world, and it may be no coincidence that this was the home of the most striking animal-style art.

The pieces in the Siberian Collection are dynamic in concept and full of expression. The composition of both large-scale and small objects is masterly and rhythmical, with details subordinated to the main design. Nowhere are there compositions so full of movement as those with two, three or even four fighting animals, their bodies intricately interlaced. Here the craftsman has succeeded in producing supremely graceful and really elegant works of art. There is a feeling of tranquillity about the twin belt-plaques with the epic scene of horsemen and their mounts resting in a wood (cat. no. 5), whilst the wild-boar hunt illustrated on another pair of plaques is dominated by movement which includes the horsemen, the quarry and even the wind-bent branches of the tree. These objects are decorative as well as pictorial. Coloured inlays, frequently of turquoise (cat. no. 10), were used with great discretion and a sense of proportion. The artists skilfully avoided monotony by using a refined stylization.

Apart from the pairs of belt-plaques the collection contains horse-harness and personal ornaments such as ear-rings, finger-rings, bracelets and pendants. Most of the objects were made in the fifth and fourth centuries BC, probably by local craftsmen working for the aristocracy, but the collection also contains some obviously imported pieces including vessels with Aramaic inscriptions, cheek-pieces from horse-harness with representations of elephants, and there is some use of motifs borrowed from Achaemenid Persia.

The entire collection is one of magnificent works of decorative applied art, whose designs are full of mythological, epic and symbolic significance.

1 Bracelet

Gold; length 23cm; diameter 9.5cm;
weight 695.8gr.
Sakic culture; 5th–4th centuries BC.
Siberian Collection of Peter the Great. Acquired
in 1716.
Hermitage. Si 1727 1/51.
Bibliography: Rudenko, 1962. pl. XI, 3, 4.

Bracelet of twelve coils of round wire, the ends
embellished with representations in the round of
a tiger attacking an elk. The figures, which are
chased, were cast separately. The extended
figures of the animals are skilfully designed to
harmonise with the elongated form of the
bracelet. The elk has a rounded muzzle with an
incised mouth and very carefully chased eyes and

its antlers, with their protruding frontal
extension, are tightly pressed back to the head
and neck. The rear of the elk's body is in the
tiger's open jaws. The tiger is portrayed with a
wide muzzle, a wrinkled lip and a small, round
ear. Its stripes are indicated by incised lines and
its tail terminates in a bird's head.

2 Belt plaque

Gold; length 15.2cm; weight 227.7gr.
Sakic culture; 5th–4th centuries BC.
Siberian Collection of Peter the Great.
Acquired in 1716.
Hermitage. Si 1727 1/10.
Bibliography: Rudenko, 1962. pl. XII, 4.

Rectangular plaque decorated with a
representation in relief of a predatory animal
attacking a snake. The animal, which is
crouching close to the ground, has the muzzle of
a wolf, clawed paws, and a long tail. Coiled
about its body is a snake with diamond-shaped
scales, probably intended to represent a grass-
snake attempting to avoid combat. The
prototype of the predator is the badger – an
animal which preys upon snakes. This was a
popular subject and is repeated on three different
plaques in the Siberian Collection.

The indentations in the frame of the plaque,
the body of the beast and the neck of the snake
were intended to hold coloured inlays. The
plaque had been broken in two and repaired in
antiquity. In order to join the pieces three pairs
of holes were bored and the fragments were

△1

2▽

joined on the reverse side with a gold plate. On the reverse is the impression of the coarse cloth with which the mould was covered and, in the region of the predator's tail, a bracket for the belt. There is a fastening hook on the neck of the snake. This plaque, one of a pair, belongs to a series of similar belt-clasps in the Siberian Collection.

3 Belt plaque
Gold; length 16.8cm; width 9.2cm; weight 566.3gr.
Sakic culture; 5th–4th centuries BC.
Siberian Collection of Peter the Great.
Acquired in 1716.
Hermitage. Si 1727 1/12.
Bibliography: Rudenko, 1962. pl. VI, 3.

This massive, cast plaque bears a scene, executed in high relief, of a battle between a tiger and a fantastic wolf-like animal. On the reverse are two loops through which the belt was passed. During the casting process holes formed in the tail and rear paw of the tiger and were closed with rivets.

The dynamic composition of this scene of fighting animals is aided by the use of openwork technique. The wolf, rearing on its hind legs, has the three-toed paws of its forelegs braced against the tiger's back and leg, and is biting the tiger's neck. The tiger's teeth are sunk in the wolf's foreleg. The realistic representation of the tiger is close in style to those found in the Altai (cat. no. 11). Its head has a wide nose and wrinkled cheeks; the contour of the eyes is emphasised by brows in relief, and the ears are semicircular. The tiger's paws have four claws and its long tail is curled in a circle at the end. The portrayal is completed by vertical marks which imitate the tiger's stripes and add impact to the figure.

The wolf has a long muzzle, a turned-up nose, and a realistically rendered ear. Its neck is decorated with four birds' heads and an identical head completes its upraised tail. The wolf's leonine body and powerful paws are well modelled and the birds have hooked beaks, round protruding eyes and rounded ears.

The cells in the ears and paws of both the animals are unfinished and did not contain inlays.
Colour plate

4 Plaque
Gold; length 10.9cm; width 9.3cm; weight 221.2gr.
Sakic culture; 5th–4th centuries BC.
Siberian Collection of Peter the Great.
Acquired in 1716.
Hermitage. Si 1727 1/88.
Bibliography: Rudenko, 1962. pl. VI, 1 and XXVI, 2 (reverse side).

Cast plaque, bearing a representation in relief of a coiled predatory animal. The animal's elongated elastic body is curved in a semicircle so that the head and tail meet. Within the circle, creating an open-work effect, are the tail and paws drawn close to the body. The circles which terminate the paws and tail originally contained inlays, as did the ear, eye and nostril and the opening of the jaws. In the workmanship sculptural modelling is skilfully combined with jeweller's techniques, in particular the soldering of the settings for inlays to the metal strip of the tail and the joining of the muzzle, paws and tail by cloisons. The cells on the paws and the end of the tail were originally open and were closed on the reverse with small scales of gold soldered on after the stones had been inset. Three rings were soldered onto the reverse of the plaque to hold the belt.

The motif of a predatory animal coiled into a circle was widespread in Scytho-Siberian art and this plaque is an example of the decorative use of the image. Earlier examples of such subjects convey the animals' predatory essence in a more naturalistic way.
Colour plate

5 Belt plaque
Gold; length 15.2cm; width 12.1cm; weight 459.3gr.
Sakic culture; 5th–4th centuries BC.
Siberian Collection of Peter the Great.
Acquired in 1716.
Hermitage. Si 1727 1/61
Bibliography: Rudenko, 1962. pl. VII, 1.

6

The scene cast in relief and painstakingly chased on this open-work plaque is unique. On the reverse can be seen the imprint of the coarse cloth with which the mould was covered during casting and three loops through which the belt was passed.

A man and a woman are seated under a tree, their legs folded under them in the 'asiatic style'. Another man is lying across their knees. The seated man holds the reins of two saddled and bridled war horses. On the tree hangs a *gorytus* (a combined quiver and bow-case) with bow and arrows.

The woman's head, seen in profile, is crowned by a high head-dress from which the two plaits of her hair rise up and are interlaced with the foliage of the tree (a similar head-dress was discovered at Pazyryk in barrow 5). Her cloak has narrow ornamental sleeves from under which one hand is touching the head of the lying man.

The men are portrayed identically with their round, moustachioed faces framed by bobbed hair. The shoulders and sleeves of their garments are decorated. The reclining warrior is dressed in a short, belted tunic and narrow trousers.

The figures of the horses and their harness are modelled with great knowledge and skill. The horses' manes are closely clipped and their tails plaited. The bridles, saddles and embellishments are similar to the original sets of harness found in the Pazyryk barrows.

The leaves on the tree, the human figures and the horses are portrayed in a state of peace and tranquillity. Possibly the subject is an illustration of a scene from an ancient epic, and may depict the resurrection of a dead warrior by his wife and his sworn battle comrade. Instances of the resurrection of a dead warrior are known in ancient Turkish epics based on the traditions of earlier times.
Colour plate

6 Belt plaque

Gold; length 12.0cm; width 7.4cm; weight 173gr.
Sakic culture; 5th–4th centuries BC.
Siberian Collection of Peter the Great.
Acquired in 1716.
Hermitage. Si 1727 1/19.
Bibliography: Rudenko, 1962. pl. VIII, 4.

7

7 Belt-slide

Gold; length 7.5cm; weight 58.3gr.
Sakic culture; 5th–4th centuries BC.
Siberian Collection of Peter the Great.
Acquired in 1716.
Hermitage. Si 1727 1/163.
Bibliography: Rudenko, 1962. pl. IV, 1.

One of a pair of plaques portraying a predatory animal similar to that represented in no. 2.

The animal has a crouching, muscular body, short legs with four-clawed paws and a long tail terminating in a bird's head. The details of the head and trunk are subtly modelled and the ear and mane are formed of leaf-shaped cells. The animal is portrayed on a background of pairs of birds' heads on curved necks. Under its muzzle are two supine birds with their beaks touching. The next four birds are facing to the right and the last two to the left. All the birds are represented identically with open beaks, elongated ears, prominent cheeks and drop-shaped eyes outlined by brows executed in relief. The cells in the animal's mane and the birds' ears are unfinished and did not contain inlays. The reverse of the plaque bears the imprint of cloth. The object was not chased.

Belt-slide decorated with the figure of a fantastic wolf crouched ready to spring with the rear paws drawn up under the body. The wolf's head, which has a long closed mouth, a turned-up nose, large protruding eyes framed by lids and brows in relief, and a well-modelled ear rests on its long-clawed fore-paws. A bird's head with a hooked beak decorates the end of the curved tail and two other similar birds' heads are located on the animal's forehead and neck.

Four identical belt-slides were found together with a pair of belt-plaques on which were portrayed a similar fantastic wolf (cat. no. 3). The object is cast and has a hollow interior. Indentations on the ears and paws of the wolf were intended to hold inlays and a broad loop is soldered to the inner face.

△8

9▽

8 Button

Gold; diameter 3.6cm; height 2.6cm;
weight 65gr.
Sakic culture; 5th–4th centuries BC.
Siberian Collection of Peter the Great.
Acquired in 1716.
Hermitage. Si 1727 1/49.
Bibliography: Rudenko, 1962. pl. XXIII, 28.

One of a pair of cast buttons with representations
in high relief of a horse coiled into a circle with
its rear legs drawn up and its forelegs extended.
The large expressive head is turned backwards
on the twisted neck and completes the upper
part of the composition. On its prominent
muzzle the incised nostrils and the line of the
mouth are painstakingly rendered. The great
semi-circular eye and large ears are also incised
and the sockets of the eyes, nostrils, ears and
hooves were intended to hold inlays. The horse's
tail protrudes between its forelegs and touches
its ear. The backs of the buttons, on which the
imprint of cloth survives, are fitted with cross-
bars.

9 Strap-end

Gold; length 6.9cm; weight 49.3gr.
Sakic culture; 5th–4th centuries BC.
Siberian Collection of Peter the Great.
Acquired in 1717.
Hermitage. Si 1727 1/23.
Bibliography: Rudenko, 1962. pl. VII, 5, 6. fig. 27.

Tapered strap-end cast with a hollow interior.
The upper end is diagonally cut away on the
reverse side and the obverse is decorated with
the closely interlaced figures of a wolf and a
mountain goat. The curved body of the goat is
unnaturally twisted: one foreleg is drawn up,
the other is extended to the head. The annual
growth rings on its large horns are represented by
semicircles. The wolf has sunk its teeth into the
goat's neck. One of its long-clawed forepaws
embraces the goat from below while the other is
near the goat's muzzle.

There are four such strap-ends in the
collection. They are remarkable for the
ingenuity with which the available space is
utilized by the composition.

10 Belt plaque

Gold and turquoise; length 15.1cm;
width 9.9cm; weight 327.8gr.
Sakic culture; 5th–4th centuries BC.
Siberian Collection of Peter the Great.
Acquired in 1717.
Hermitage. Si 1727 1/3.
Bibliography: Rudenko, 1962. pl. I, 4.

Plaque with a representation in relief of a yak,
an eagle and a tiger fighting. This is one of the
most expressive and complicated belt plaques in
the Siberian Collection of Peter the Great. An
eared eagle is shown biting and clawing a yak
which, in its turn, is goring a tiger. The tiger is
biting the eagle's tail which it holds with one
front paw. The figure of the yak, magnificently
portrayed in realistic detail, has its head bent to
the ground, and its curved tongue can be seen in
the open mouth. Its eye, nostril and ear are
rounded, and its body, tail and mane are covered
with long, undulating wool. The hooves,
pasterns, eye, nostril and ear are each decorated
with turquoise inlays.

The powerful figure of the eagle, standing on
the yak's horns, is also very realistic. Its head,
with hooked beak and great eye, is particularly
expressive. The plumage on the body and legs is
indicated by a design of diamond shapes.
Turquoise inlays at the lower ends of the wing
feathers and in the ear and eye accentuate the
decorative and expressive qualities of the figure.

The tiger is shown in a complicated twisted
pose. Its head, visible above and behind the
eagle's tail, is turned backwards, showing its
wide nose, wrinkled muzzle, one large semi-oval
ear, and an eye executed in relief. Its body forms
an elipse while its curved tail passes behind the
yak's head. The tiger's body is modelled with
incised, sharp-ridged grooves imitating stripes
and its eye and ear are inlaid with turquoise.

The reverse of the plaque bears the imprint of
the cloth used during the casting process, and
there are two loops for the belt in the region of
the yak's hind legs. The turquoise inlays have
holes bored through them, indicating that they
have been previously used in other objects.
Colour plate

THE FROZEN TOMBS OF THE ALTAI

Catalogue numbers 11–102

The most important part of the exhibition consists of objects from the frozen barrows of the High Altai. The story of the discovery of this culture begins early in the nineteenth century when a local *savant*, P. K. Frolov, began to collect antiquities including wooden and bone pieces decorated in the animal style (cat. nos. 75–77). These objects, mainly horse-harness decorations, had been plundered from barrows in the Altai. In 1865 Academician V. V. Radlov, then a teacher in the school at Barnaul, excavated two large barrows in the High Altai, at Katanda and Berel. As permafrost had formed under the stone cairns, fur garments and objects of wood and birch-bark had been preserved in the graves, but Radlov did not fully excavate them and the material he recovered was not adequately dated or ascribed. However, Frolov's collection and the results of Radlov's excavations were to be correctly interpreted when Soviet archaeologists undertook new and significant excavations of the Altai barrows.

The expedition of what was then the Archaeological Section of the Russian Museum began its archaeological work in the High Altai under the direction of S. I. Rudenko in the 1920s. In 1927 the young Leningrad archaeologist M. P. Gryaznov, excavated a large barrow at the Shibe site which produced interesting finds and confirmed the presence of frozen ground under the stone cairns. Two years later the same expedition excavated a barrow in the centre of a chain of five large burial mounds at Pazyryk, in the eastern Altai some 1600 metres above sea-level. In 1947–49, Rudenko, at the head of an expedition of the Institute of Archaeology of the Academy of Sciences and the State Hermitage Museum, completed the excavation of the other four Pazyryk barrows and transferred his operations to the Central Altai where, in 1950, he excavated two mounds at Bashadar, and in 1954 two more at Tuekta. All these barrows were frozen and they produced the world-famous finds from which we know the strikingly original culture of these early nomads. This research is still in progress, for young archaeologists of the Siberian Section of the Academy of Sciences of the USSR at Novosibirsk are now excavating the smaller barrows.

The Altai barrows have achieved world-wide fame because, being completely frozen, they preserved objects made of organic materials which, in normal conditions, are soon destroyed by the passage of time. Amongst the finds were articles of fur and leather, felt and textile, as well as wood-carvings, and all of them had retained their original form and colour.

The excavated barrows had been constructed more or less in the same way. First, a rectangular pit was dug, from four to seven metres deep, in which was set a chamber of larch-logs, often with double walls, a ceiling and a plank floor. In the chamber was a coffin, hollowed out of a trunk of centuries-old larch, and inside were laid the mummified bodies of the tribal chieftain and his wife or concubine. Accompanying the dead was a rich assemblage of grave-goods: clothing, vessels holding food and drink, small tables (which could be converted into dishes), wooden pillows, carpets, multi-stringed harps, and weapons – everything that was believed to be necessary in the afterlife. Fully caparisoned riding horses, sometimes with fantastic masks on their heads, were slaughtered and their bodies buried outside the chamber. In one barrow there was also the dismantled parts of a ceremonial carriage (Rudenko 1970: pl. 131). After the burial the pit was covered with layers of birch-bark and twigs of *dasiphora fruticosa* (shrubby cinquefoil), followed by layers of larch logs. Then the soil previously excavated from the pit was piled on top and covered by a cairn of stones up to sixty metres in diameter and four to five metres high.

Soon after the burial a lens-shaped area of frozen ground developed under the cairn. The stones of the cairn had been piled loosely, and they prevented the soil from heating in summer whilst in winter they helped the intense frost to penetrate to the bottom of the grave and establish there a constant sub-zero temperature. Any water which seeped into the grave froze before it could rot the objects of organic origin. The refrigeration in the mounds was also assisted by cavities in the burial chambers, and by the severe climate of the High Altai, where the winters are long with little snow and the summers short with night frosts.

The timbers from the barrows have been subjected to dendrochronological and carbon-14 determinations which have produced consistent results showing

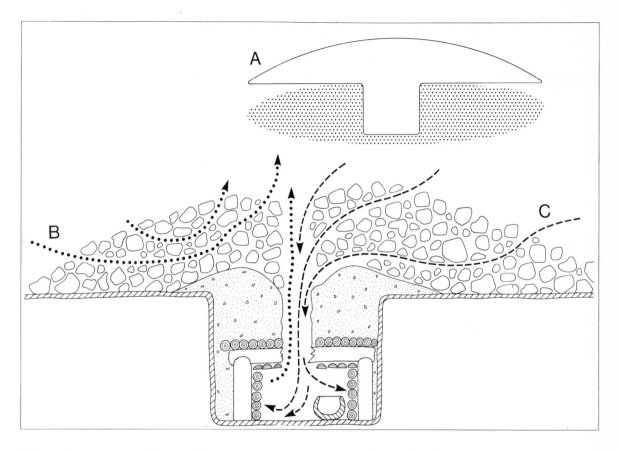

Above Schematic section of a typical frozen tomb in the Altai. **A** A lens of permafrost forms beneath the great stone mound. **B** The warm air rises and as it is cooled by the stones of the cairn surplus moisture is deposited. **C** The cold air sinks, driving out the warm air and freezing everything.

Opposite General view of a stone cairn covering a frozen tomb at Pazyryk.

that the excavated barrows were constructed between the sixth and fourth centuries BC.

The finds from the Altai barrows enable us to reconstruct the customs and rites of the magnificent funeral of a chieftain. The funeral took place in the cold season of early spring or autumn. The bodies were embalmed, the muscle tissues removed through incisions in the skin and the cavities left filled with grass before the incisions were sewn up with sinews. The skulls were trepanned to remove the brains (cat. no. 27). After the funeral there was a feast and a ritual cleansing by fumigation with the smoke of hemp seeds. Small tents were built of thin rods covered by a rug, and bronze censers filled with heated stones were placed inside (cat. no. 32). The mourners then clambered into the tent, threw hemp seeds onto the heated stones and inhaled the narcotic smoke. These funeral practices in the Altai correspond to descriptions of similar rites among the Scythians of the Black Sea region in the fifth century BC. Herodotus' account of the custom of scalping enemies and the tattooing of the bravest and most renowned warriors are also confirmed (cat. no. 31). Other beliefs and superstitions are illustrated by finds of amulet-pouches containing roots of plants and herbs, locks of hair and nail-pairings.

The burials in the Altai barrows were of chieftains or war-lords, owners of large numbers of domestic animals – the main form of wealth as well as providing all the essentials of life: food, drink, leather, fur and wool. Domestic animals and the pelts of wild animals were probably the medium of exchange in trade with neighbouring tribes.

The ancient inhabitants of the Altai produced leather of various qualities, the finest of which was used for delicate appliqué work, whilst thick leather was employed in bridle straps and three-dimensional details of sculpture. They were aware of several stitches, and made skilful use of them for decoration. From both coarse and fine sheep's wool they made felt of different densities, qualities and thicknesses which was widely used in everyday life and in art. Flat polychrome appliqué work such as the sculptural figures of swans (cat. nos. 34 and 35) was fashioned from felt.

Textiles were made of sheep's wool or, more accurately, down. Serges are represented in great variety, and a particular favourite was one with four warp threads, very close in structure to plaited weaves. In contrast to the polychrome imported textiles the local Altai cloths were always of one colour, generally red. Serge was used to upholster saddle-bows, to make the strips of a coverlet (cat. no. 41), and the soles of a woman's dress bootees (cat. no. 23). Textiles with a long pile were also popular and were possibly used as carpets (cat. no. 42). They were woven both with whole and with cut loops – with the loops cut their quantity was more than doubled and the density of the pile was increased.

Linen-type textiles of the simplest manufacture, both soft and coarse, were used to upholster a variety of things.

Plaited-weave and lace-weave textiles from the Altai barrows resemble those known from Siberia as early as the fifteenth century BC. Evidently the intensive development of weaving did not displace plaiting, which was used in the Altai mainly for decorative trims such as ribbons, laces and tassels. The history of lace-weaving was almost 1000 years old when the woman's pigtail-cover (cat. no. 26), a fine example of complicated patterned lace, was made by an Altai craftswoman.

Men's shirts woven from vegetable fibres of *kendyr*, the Siberian hemp which grows in the Altai, were also discovered in the barrows. *Kendyr* is still used for weaving among the modern tribes of Siberia, but doubt has been cast on the local manufacture of these ancient shirts because of their high quality of workmanship and because vegetable materials were rarely used by the early nomads.

The imported fabrics are invaluable for the study of the history of weaving techniques. Delicate textiles of tapestry type, decorated with intricate and elegant designs in many colours, came from the Middle East. These textiles were highly valued in antiquity, but they have been preserved only in the Altai barrows. They are double-sided and not less than 60cm wide. The strip of tapestry with figures of lions (cat. no. 40) is part of a cloth with three different designs (see A. A. Gavrilova's reconstruction which is published here, overleaf, for the first time). A second tapestry, with a design of geometric figures, is probably also of Middle Eastern origin. It is coarser than the lion strip, but also has a polychrome design. The coverlet (cat. no. 41) was sewn with strips of this fabric alternating with strips of local serge. The Middle East is also the home of the world's most ancient carpet (Rudenko 1970: pls. 174–5), whose rich polychrome design is carried out in the *ghiordes* knotted technique.

Highly prized silk textiles were occasionally used to trim articles belonging to the Altai aristocracy. As well as linen-weave silk – taffeta – there is a fragment of intricately designed repp which is probably from a garment, and monochrome repp embroidered in tambour-work was used to trim a horse's saddle-blanket (cat. no. 39). The inhabitants of the Altai imported fabrics by the piece and then cut them as required to make their own articles – sometimes disregarding the original design.

Nowhere else is there such a complete record of the early nomads' vivid and original animal-style as that from the frozen barrows of the Altai. The works of art from these aristocratic burials were created by fellow tribesmen, craftsmen with the accumulated experience of many generations of popular art. This was 'applied art' in the widest sense of the term. The people of the Altai decorated everything they used: clothing, footwear, vessels, utensils, weapons, horse-

◁ p.25

trappings, living-quarters and furniture. Their art was decorative, ornate and extremely colourful for they loved pure, contrasting colours – red, blue, yellow and green. A considerable number of objects made of leather, fur and felt were decorated with polychrome appliqué-work and embroidery using designs of vegetable and geometrical inspiration.

Frequent use was made of animal motifs, with tigers, wolves, deer, elk, mountain sheep and goats, birds of prey and domestic fowl depicted in a variety of materials. Representations of men, horses, hares, boars and *saiga* antelopes are more rarely found. The figures of fantastic birds and beasts such as horned tigers and large-eared gryphons with cocks' combs, are exceptionally powerful, and sometimes these are shown fighting with real animals. In their representations of animals, and also as quite separate designs, the artists made bold use of volutes, spirals and other geometric devices as well as vegetable-derived motifs such as lotus flowers and palmettes.

The wood-carvers of the Altai were highly accomplished in all forms of sculpture: high and low relief, incised design and three-dimensional work. In a single object they would cleverly combine several materials, including wood, leather, paint, and sheet-gold or -tin sheathing. In relief carvings they would sometimes attach separate three-dimensional details. Decorated objects are skilfully composed, with the design adapted to the form without the least constraint.

The art of the Altai is most closely related on the one hand to the pieces in the Siberian Collection of Peter the Great, and on the other to the art of Tuva.

11

11 Lid of a coffin

Wood; length 315cm; width 50cm.
Central Altai, Bashadar, barrow 2. Excavations
of S. I. Rudenko, 1950.
Early nomadic culture; 6th century BC.
Hermitage. 1793/1.
Bibliography: Rudenko, 1970. p. 269.

Coffin-lid of larch wood, the surface decorated
with carvings of eleven animals. Four snarling
jawed tigers with powerful clawed paws and the
ends of their tails curled into a circle are shown
walking in procession. The texture of their fur is
indicated by incised zig-zag lines. Under the
tigers' feet are four animals in calm poses, three
lying at rest – two mountain rams and an elk –
and one standing – a boar (an exceptionally rare
subject in the art of the ancient Altai). Three
other animals are shown in energetic movement
– a mountain ram running with its head turned
back, a boar preparing to spring, and an elk in
headlong flight, its body so violently curved that
its hind legs are extended at an angle of almost
180 degrees to its forelegs – a characteristic pose
in Altai art. All the figures are treated
ornamentally with a strong decorative effect
created by the rows of energetically drawn lines
and the rhythm of the vortices and scrolls by
which the whole composition is enlivened and
imbued with movement.

12 Small table

Wood; length of legs 36.7cm; top 64.5 × 51.5cm.
High Altai, Pazyryk, barrow 2. Excavations
of S. I. Rudenko, 1947.
Early nomadic culture; 5th century BC.
Hermitage. 1684/35.
Bibliography: Rudenko, 1970. pl. 50A.

One of the best examples of the furniture of the
early nomads of the Altai.

The top is made of a single piece of wood and
was coloured red with cinnabar (preserved only
on the underside). The underside is convex with
four short stumps each with a socket into which
a leg was fitted. The legs are carved in the shape
of tigers standing on their hind legs and
supporting the table-top with their forelegs
and muzzles.

The animals' muzzles are carefully modelled

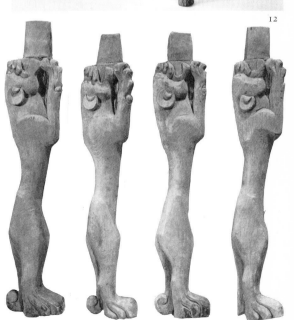

12

with almond-shaped eyes, ears carved in relief with a scroll at their base, and snarling, predatory jaws. As the legs were not cut from a pattern each one is slightly different from the others. The table is collapsible: the top could easily be removed and turned into a large dish – a convenience in a nomadic way of life.

13

13 Wooden pillow with leather case
Wood, leather, fur; length of pillow 39.5cm; greatest width 19.5cm; height 11.5cm; length of case 35.5cm
High Altai, Pazyryk, barrow 2. Excavations of S. I. Rudenko, 1947.
Early nomadic culture, 5th century BC.
Hermitage. 1684/33–34.
Bibliography: Rudenko, 1970. pl. 53B.

Wooden pillow or head-rest of oval form with a slight waist in the middle. The surface was dressed with an axe, the marks still easily visible. A special case of leather and fur had been drawn over the pillow. The case survives as a fragment, elegantly decorated with applied coloured leather cut-outs. Pillows of this kind were found in all the large Altai barrows.

14 Wooden stake
Wood; length 71cm; diameter c. 4cm.
High Altai, Pazyryk, barrow 4. Excavations of S. I. Rudenko, 1948.
Early nomadic culture; 5th–4th centuries BC.
Hermitage. 1686/171.
Bibliography: Rudenko, 1970. pl. 36c.

A stake with its lower end cut in the shape of a wedge. The upper end has been flattened by blows from a mallet. Such wedges were used to loosen the earth when grave pits were being dug in hard ground.

15 Mallet
Wood; length 55cm; width 13cm.
High Altai, Pazyryk, barrow 2. Excavations of S. I. Rudenko, 1947.
Early nomadic culture; 5th century BC.
Hermitage. 1684/533.
Bibliography: Rudenko, 1970. pl. 37A.

A massive mallet with a long handle, made from the root of a larch tree. The end of the handle had been crookedly trimmed and later broken. The head of the mallet is dented by use.

16 Shovel
Wood; length 127cm; width 10cm.
High Altai, Pazyryk, barrow 2. Excavations of S. I. Rudenko, 1947.
Early nomadic culture; 5th century BC.
Hermitage. 1684/539.
Bibliography: Rudenko, 1970. pl. 36B.

A wooden shovel with a long, narrow and slightly curved blade and a long round-sectioned handle. Such shovels were used to dig out and fill the grave pits and to pile up the mound of earth.

17 Bottle
Earthenware; height 50cm; diameter of mouth 18cm; maximum diameter of body 29cm.
High Altai, Pazyryk, barrow 2. Excavations of S. I. Rudenko, 1947.
Early nomadic culture; 5th century BC.
Hermitage, 1684/53.
Bibliography: Rudenko, 1970. pl. 55B.

A narrow mouthed bottle of a type characteristic of the ancient nomads of the Altai. In nomadic conditions, such vessels are convenient as they can be transported without spilling the contents. They were used to contain water, *kumys* (fermented mare's-milk) and other liquids. The bottle, made of coarse clay with a significant admixture of sand, was built up by placing rings of clay one upon another, not thrown on a potter's wheel. The firing was uneven, being carried out over an open fire. The inner and outer surfaces are covered by a well levigated reddish-yellow slip.

△15   17▽

14   16

△18

19 ▽

18 Felt ring

Felt; length 34.5cm; maximum width 20cm.
High Altai, Pazyryk, barrow 2. Excavations
of S. I. Rudenko, 1947.
Early nomadic culture; 5th century BC.
Hermitage. 1684/50, 52.
Bibliography: Rudenko, 1970. p. 70, fig. 21.

This ring, made of twisted strips of thick black
felt tightly wrapped in fine red felt, was sewn
to a decorated felt coverlet and used as a stand
for an earthenware pot. The pot was placed
inside the ring for greater stability.

19 Bottle

Leather; height 23cm; maximum width 11cm.
High Altai, Pazyryk, barrow 2. Excavations
of S. I. Rudenko, 1947.
Early nomadic culture; 5th century BC.
Hermitage 1684/93.
Bibliography: Rudenko, 1970. pl. 152B.

This bottle, made of four strips of carefully
dressed leather sewn together with sinew
threads, was used to hold seeds or roots of
medicinal herbs. It is decorated with an elegant
plant design of applied finely-dressed leather
dyed a red-brown colour.

   Various decorations composed of geometrical
and plant motifs played an important part in the
art of the ancient inhabitants of the Altai and
were employed in leather, felt and fur appliqués.

20 Man's shirt

Textile; length 108cm; width at hem 130cm;
width at shoulders 93cm; width of
material 44.5cm.
High Altai, Pazyryk, barrow 2. Excavations
of S. I. Rudenko, 1947.
Early nomadic culture; 5th century BC.
Hermitage. 1684/194.
Bibliography: Rudenko, 1970. pl. 63.

This man's shirt is a rare example of the clothing
of the ancient inhabitants of the Altai. The cloth
is a linen-weave material of *kendyr* (hemp)
fibres, originally white, now faded to grey by
the passage of time. One half of the garment is
of a finer and lighter-coloured material than the
other, which is darker and coarser. The sleeves

20

were sewn on without gussets but four gussets were sewn in below the hem at the sides. The main seams of the shirt, the cuffs of the sleeves and the collar were bound with fine red woollen braid and cord.

21 Head-dress

Felt, leather, lacquer; height 34.5cm.
High Altai, Pazyryk, barrow 3. Excavations
of S. I. Rudenko, 1948.
Early nomadic culture; 5th–4th centuries BC.
Hermitage. 1689/16.
Bibliography: Rudenko, 1970. pl. 155B.

Man's head-dress with a round crown and long
side flaps, made of two pieces of white felt
joined together in the middle by a single seam.
The felt crown is covered by thin, finely-dressed
leather. The whole head-dress is edged with a
piping of leather thong. Beside the flaps,
traces of some kind of decoration have been
preserved, coloured red and with the remains of
dark-red lacquer. The top of the head-dress is
embellished with a square 'towerlet' of four
identical shapes cut from thick leather.

22 Fragment of a belt-strap

Leather; length 53cm; width 5.7cm.
High Altai, Pazyryk, barrow 2. Excavations
of S. I. Rudenko, 1947.
Early nomadic culture; 5th century BC.
Hermitage. 1684/241.
Bibliography: Rudenko, 1970. p. 100, fig. 42.

Fragment of a belt-strap, its outer face trimmed
with thin leather. To the leather are attached five
figures of cocks, cut out of thick leather in low
relief. The bodies, tails and combs of the cocks
are decorated with ornamental cut-outs in the
shape of triangles, full stops and half-horseshoes.
This distinctive stylistic device is important in
the art of the ancient Altai and is characteristic
also of Middle Eastern art.

22

21

39 △

△ 36

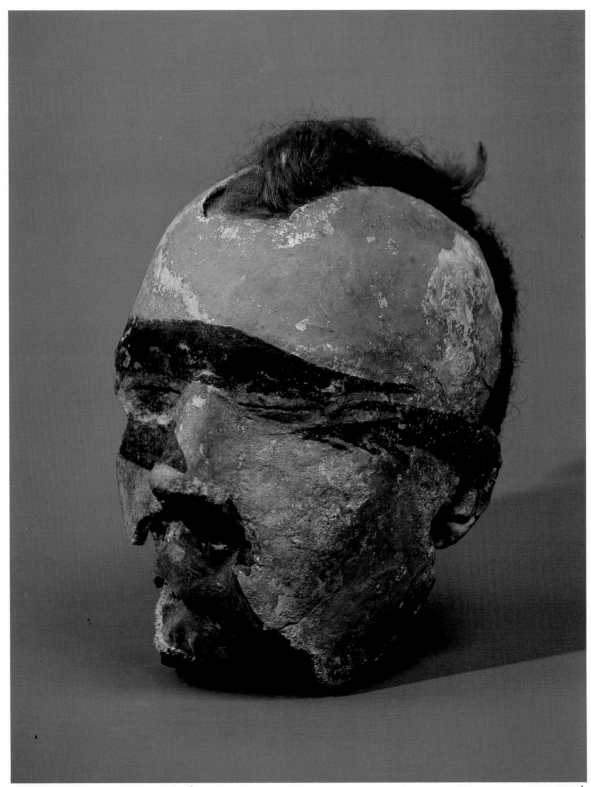

23

24

23 Bootee

Leather, textile, tin, gold; height 36cm;
length of sole 19cm.
High Altai, Pazyryk, barrow 2. Excavations
of S. I. Rudenko, 1947.
Early nomadic culture; 5th century BC.
Hermitage. 1684/218.
Bibliography: Rudenko, 1970. pl. 64A.

This bootee of soft leather with a short, flaring
top, was not sewn up at the heel and covered
only the front of the shin. The vamp is made of
a single piece of leather and sewn to the sole
with sinew threads in such a way that the front
part of the toe is crimped into fine pleats. The
sole is embroidered with beads and 84 small
cubes of pyrites, a golden-silvery mineral. The
vamp is entirely ornamented with appliqués of
red, finely dressed leather, and the embroidered
decoration is executed in sinew thread wrapped
in tin-foil. The main motif of the ornament, the
lotus flower, is repeated in intricate and elegant
combinations. It is essentially a Middle Eastern
design but here it is given local variations.

24 Stocking

Felt; length 82cm.
High Altai, Pazyryk, barrow 2. Excavations
of S. I. Rudenko, 1947.
Early nomadic culture; 5th century BC.
Hermitage. 1684/221.
Bibliography: Rudenko, 1970. p. 88, fig. 31.

A man's long stocking cut from a single piece of
white felt and sewn together with fine sinew
thread with two seams – one along the edge of
the sole and one up the back of the stocking
from the top to the heel. The toe of the stocking
is pleated where it is sewn to the short,
narrow sole.

△25

26 ▷

25 Sock

Felt; length 44cm.
High Altai, Pazyryk, barrow 2. Excavations
of S. I. Rudenko, 1947.
Early nomadic culture; 5th century BC.
Hermitage. 1684/224.
Bibliography: Rudenko, 1970. p. 98, fig. 40.

Sock made of two pieces of white felt sewn
together by fine sinew thread with only three
seams: a short seam up the back, a curved seam
over the instep and a third seam along the edge
of the sole. The vamp, which was cut from a
single piece of felt, is gathered into fine pleats
where it is sewn to the narrow sole. The upper
edge is scalloped. From the circumstances of the
find it appears that the socks were worn with the
woman's bootees (cat. no. 23) and were left in
them when not in use.

26 Pigtail-case

Wool; length 18.5cm.
High Altai, Pazyryk, barrow 2. Excavations
of S. I. Rudenko, 1947.
Early nomadic culture; 5th century BC.
Hermitage. 1684/242.
Bibliography: Rudenko, 1970. pl. 133F.

Case for a woman's pigtail, woven in lace-weave
in dark-red wool. The case consisted of two
cylindrical nets, one inside the other, drawn into
a cone and tied together at one end. The outer
case is exhibited.

27 Mummified head of a man

Height of head 25cm.
High Altai, Pazyryk, barrow 2. Excavations
of S. I. Rudenko, 1947.
Early nomadic culture; 5th century BC.
Hermitage. 1684/297.
Bibliography: Rudenko, 1970. pl. 44A.

This head of a chieftain had been hacked off by
tomb-robbers and was found outside the coffin
and separate from the body. The head is severely
damaged: the crown is pierced by three holes
made by a battle-axe – two in the right parietal
bone and one in the left. There are also marks of
the trepanning carried out after death to remove
the brain. On the right temple is a wound about

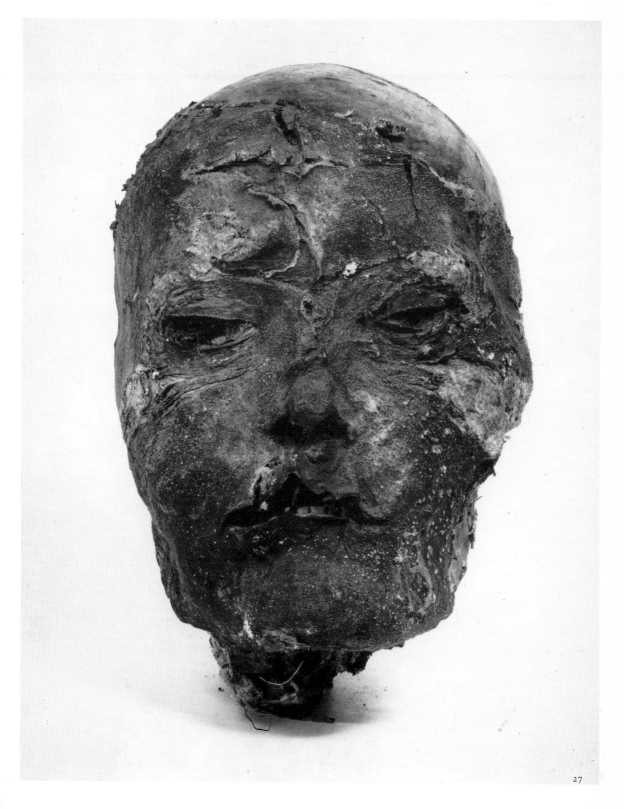

27

28

3cm long which had been carefully sewn together with fine sinew thread. The corpse had been scalped. The worn state of the teeth indicates that death occurred at the age of about sixty. The corpse is of an obviously mongoloid physical type. The hair of the head and eyebrows has not been preserved, but on the cheeks, which had been shaved several days before death, stiff black hairs can easily be seen. This body was tattooed (see cat. no. 31).

28 Mirror with horn handle

Silver, horn; diameter 15cm; length of handle 11.5cm.
High Altai, Pazyryk, barrow 2. Excavations of S. I. Rudenko, 1947.
Early nomadic culture; 5th century BC.
Hermitage. 1684/89.
Bibliography: Rudenko, 1970. pl. 70A.

Silver mirror made in two halves fastened together with seven rivets. The obverse is completely smooth with a pointed metal tang which is fitted into a handle of ox-horn. The reverse has a circular ridge around the edge, a lower ridge within it and a projecting cone in the centre; it is decorated with geometrical ornament.

29 Fragment of mirror

(Chinese, of the so-called Tsin type)
White metal; diameter 11.5cm; thickness 1mm.
High Altai, Pazyryk, barrow 6. Excavations of S. I. Rudenko, 1949.
Early nomadic culture; 4th century BC.
Hermitage. 2063/9.
Bibliography: Rudenko, 1970. pl. 70c.

Fragment of a mirror. The obverse is polished and the reverse is decorated, and has a small lug in the centre. The ornament on the reverse, which is executed in relief, consists of the so-called 'wings and feathers' pattern, amongst which four shapes stand out in the form of a capital T.

The mirror was probably used not only for everyday purposes but also as a ritual article, possessing a magic power which protected its owner from evil spirits.

29

30

30 Shield

Wood, leather; length 35.5cm; width 27.5cm.
High Altai, Pazyryk, barrow 1. Excavations
of M. P. Gryaznov, 1929.
Early nomadic culture; 5th century BC.
Hermitage. 1295/232.
Bibliography: Rudenko, 1970. pl. 144C.

An example of Altai defensive weaponry.
The shield is rectangular and consists of thirty-
five round sticks held together by a piece of thin
leather. The sticks are threaded through slits in
the leather forming an interlaced effect
resembling a textile with a diamond-shaped
design. On the reverse there is a broad leather
loop. Shields are normally found among the
buried horses and they generally appear to have
been fastened to the right side of the saddle.

31 Tattoo from a chieftain's arm

Skin; length 60cm; maximum width 28cm.
High Altai, Pazyryk, barrow 2. Excavations
of S. I. Rudenko, 1947.
Early nomadic culture; 5th century BC.
Hermitage. 1684/298.
Bibliography: Rudenko, 1970. p. 111, fig. 53, 54.

The body of the chieftain was covered by
tattoos produced by deep pricking into which
a black colouring substance was introduced. The
tattoos on the right arm were particularly well
preserved. Here is a whole series of designs:
a wild ass, a fantastic winged beast with a feline
tail, a mountain ram and a deer with a bird's
beak – all of them full of expression and
movement. Conventions characteristic of the
Scytho-Siberian animal style were used, including the twisting of an animal's body through 180
degrees.
   The presence of tattoos on this body indicates
the high social position of the deceased during
his life.
Colour plate

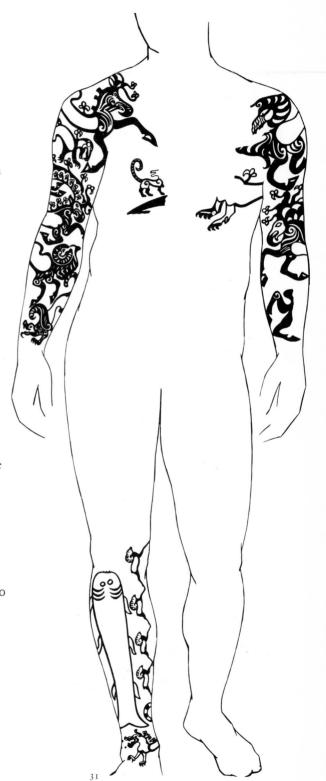

31

△32

33 ▽

32 Censer

Bronze, birch bark, stone; height 13.8cm;
maximum diameter 9.8cm.
High Altai, Pazyryk, barrow 2. Excavations of
S. I. Rudenko, 1947.
Early nomadic culture; 5th century BC.
Hermitage. 1684/122.
Bibliography: Rudenko, 1970. pl. 62B.

Censer shaped like a Scythian cauldron, with a
spherical body and a flared pedestal. Large
handles, wrapped in birch-bark, are welded onto
the sides. The vessel is filled with scorched stones
and the discovery of charred hemp seeds among
them indicates that the censer was used for
smoking narcotics (hashish). This rite is
described by Herodotus, who tells how the
Scythians threw hemp seeds on heated stones
and inhaled the smoke.

33 Tambourine-drum

Horn; height 17.2cm; maximum width 11.8cm.
High Altai, Pazyryk, barrow 2. Excavations
of S. I. Rudenko, 1947.
Early nomadic culture; 5th century BC.
Hermitage. 1684/124.
Bibliography: Rudenko, 1970. p. 278, fig. 138.

A one-sided goblet-shaped drum made of two
curved plates of ox-horn. The plates are joined
together by thread passed through minute holes
about 1mm in diameter. All the seams were
concealed by narrow gold platelets, decorated
with a twisted design, which were glued onto
them. The membrane originally stretched over
the wider upper end has not survived, but
traces of it remain in the form of a narrow white
strip. The numerous finds of drums of this type
indicate their wide use in the Altai at this period.

34, 35 Figures of swans

Felt; lengths 30cm and 27cm.
High Altai, Pazyryk, barrow 5. Excavations
of S. I. Rudenko, 1949.
Early nomadic culture; 5th–4th centuries BC.
Hermitage. 1687/260, 261.
Bibliography: Rudenko, 1970. pl. 166.

Sculptural figures of swans made of coloured
felt stuffed with deer hair. The ancient

craftsman has skilfully represented the bird's flexible, elegant neck, freely hanging wings, and fan-shaped tail. Wooden pins inserted into the small feet supported the figures in a vertical position. These are unique examples of soft sculpture. It is presumed that four such figures embellished a canopy over a grave or crowned a ceremonial carriage.

36 Saddle cover

Felt, leather, fur, hair, gold; length 119cm; width 60cm.
High Altai, Pazyryk, barrow 1. Excavations of M. P. Gryaznov, 1929.
Early nomadic culture; 5th century BC.
Hermitage. 1295/150.
Bibliography: Rudenko, 1970. pl. 135A, B.

This saddle cover is decorated with two polychrome compositions each of which depicts a scene full of vigorous movement in which an eagle-like gryphon attacks a mountain goat. Attached to the edges of the cover are pendants decorated with stylised rams' heads and horned tigers and trimmed with horsehair which has been dyed red.
Colour plate

35

37

38

37 Saddle blanket
Felt; length 265cm; width 71cm.
High Altai, Pazyryk, barrow 5. Excavations
of S. I. Rudenko, 1949.
Early nomadic culture; 5th–4th centuries BC.
Hermitage. 1687/97.
Bibliography: Rudenko, 1970. pl. 160.

Saddle blanket (shabrack) of fine white felt.
Almost the entire surface is decorated with
appliqués of coloured felt and only the narrow
strip under the saddle is not ornamented. Each
ornament is a complicated design composed of
five stylised deer antlers, their roots coming
together in a circle where they are sewn to the
felt of the blanket. The branches of the antlers
are left free and so stand away from the surface,
creating the impression of a fantastic flower with
carved petals. The heart of each 'flower' is a blue
circle with a red cross in the centre. It is
interesting to note that the pieces of coloured
felt were not sewn one over another in layers
but edge to edge, creating a coloured mosaic.

The borders of the blanket are framed with an
ornamental frieze of stylised lotus flowers and
separate deer antlers.

38 Strip of appliqué work
Felt; length 68.5cm; width 10.5cm.
High Altai, Pazyryk, barrow 2. Excavations
of S. I. Rudenko, 1947.
Early nomadic culture; 5th century BC.
Hermitage. 1684/261.
Bibliography: Rudenko, 1970. pl. 148B.

Fragment of the border of a felt carpet decorated
with an applied garland of stylised flowers and
buds of the lotus (the sacred plant of Egypt and
India). This plant motif, which reached the Altai
from the art of the Near and Middle East, is here
given a local interpretation.

39 Saddle blanket covered with Chinese silk
Felt, silk, gold, leather, hair; length 226cm;
width 65cm; width of silk 44cm; with 40×52
threads per square cm.
High Altai, Pazyryk, barrow 5. Excavations of
S. I. Rudenko, 1949.
Early nomadic culture; 5th–4th centuries BC.
Hermitage. 1687/101.
Bibliography: Rudenko, 1970. p. 175, fig. 89.

A rich silk tussore-type textile of linen weave.
On a cream coloured background in threads of
four colours (now faded but originally sand-
colour, brown, light blue and crimson) is an
embroidered design of spreading Wu T'ung
trees with elegant birds or phoenixes sitting in
their branches. Such textiles were highly prized
not only in the Altai but also in China where
they were produced for the aristrocracy, in
particular for princesses on their marriage. The
textile is sewn onto a felt saddle blanket.
Colour plate

40 Horse's chest strap
Wool, textile, fur, gold; length 80cm;
width 7cm.
High Altai, Pazyryk, barrow 5. Excavations
of S. I. Rudenko, 1949.
Early nomadic culture; 5th–4th centuries BC.
Hermitage. 1687/100.
Bibliography: Rudenko, 1970. p. 298, fig. 140.

Horse's chest strap of felt on which is sewn a
narrow strip of Iranian woollen tapestry. The
design represents fifteen figures of lions, their
shoulders and haunches picked out with
coloured circles and arcs. They are shown
walking in procession with measured tread and
in detail resemble the lions in Achaemenid
reliefs, incised gems and carvings.

40

△41

42 ▽

41 Coverlet

Woollen textile; length 252cm; width 80cm.
High Altai, Pazyryk, barrow 2. Excavations
of S. I. Rudenko, 1947.
Early nomadic culture; 5th century BC.
Hermitage. 1684/244.
Bibliography: Rudenko, 1970. pl. 157A, B.

Coverlet of three strips of red and three strips of
patterned textile. The polychrome patterned
strips are woven of yellow, red, purple and blue
threads. The combination of thick warp threads,
coarse uncoloured wool, and much thinner weft
threads produces a rhythmical pattern in the
design. Although the weft threads are combined
with the warp according to the principle of linen
weave, the different fineness and density of the
two produces a textile of the *kilim* (or, as it is
also called, weft repp) type. The red strips are of
serge weave with a diagonal pattern. The ends
of the strips are hemmed with woollen thread.

42 Fragment of a rug

Wool, textile; length 120cm; width 60cm.
High Altai, Pazyryk, barrow 2. Excavations
of S. I. Rudenko, 1947.
Early nomadic culture; 5th century BC.
Hermitage. 1684/3.
Bibliography: Rudenko, 1970. pl. 134C.

A shaggy rug woven of woollen threads. Its
present coffee colour is quite different from its
original red-brown tint. The threads are interlaced
in simple linen-weave, the weft threads being
drawn out in loops to form a pile. This pile rug,
a local Altai product, could be used either as an
underblanket or a coverlet.

43 Coffin-decoration – silhouettes of cocks

Leather; height 12cm; width 17cm.
High Altai, Pazyryk, barrow 1. Excavations
of M. P. Gryaznov, 1929.
Early nomadic culture; 5th century BC.
Hermitage. 1295/43.
Bibliography: Rudenko, 1970. p. 30, fig. 10.

Open-work leather appliqué in the form of a
pair of symmetrically arranged cocks, standing
in profile and joined at the breast. Their heads,
with beautifully outlined combs and small

△43

44▽

wattles, are turned away from each other towards their raised, fluffed-out tails.

44 Coffin-decoration – silhouettes of cocks

Leather; height 15cm; width 16.5cm.
High Altai, Pazyryk, barrow 1. Excavations of M. P. Gryaznov, 1929.
Early nomadic culture; 5th century BC.
Hermitage. 1295/51.
Bibliography: Rudenko, 1970. p. 30, fig. 10.

Silhouette leather appliqué in the form of a pair of heraldically opposed stylised cocks with elegant heads, outspread open-work wings and ornamentally cut-out tails.

45

46

45, 46 Silhouettes of cocks – decoration on a jug

Leather; dimensions 13.2 × 13.7cm, and 10.8 × 10.6cm.
High Altai, Pazyryk, barrow 2. Excavations of S. I. Rudenko, 1947.
Early nomadic culture; 5th century BC.
Hermitage. 1684/56, 57.
Bibliography: Rudenko, 1970. p. 72, fig. 22.

Silhouettes of a cock cut from thick leather. The characteristic features of the bird – the head with its comb and wattle and the upraised tail – are conveyed with great skill. Six of these silhouettes had been pasted around an earthenware vessel, the inner side of the leather covered with tinfoil facing outwards. As a stencil had not been used the figures are not identical. It is interesting that the tail of one figure had been damaged and reinforced in antiquity with a double stitch in woollen thread.

47, 48 Silhouettes of elks – decorations on a coffin

Leather; lengths 27cm and 26.5cm; width 29cm.
High Altai, Pazyryk, barrow 2. Excavations of S. I. Rudenko, 1947.
Early nomadic culture; 5th century BC.
Hermitage. 1684/285, 283.
Bibliography: Rudenko, 1970. p. 31, fig. 11.

Appliqué silhouettes of elks cut from thick leather. The appearance of the animal – the short, strong neck, the head with its long ears, the heavy upper lip and the great, spade-like antlers – is conveyed with great skill. The silhouette is relieved by triangular openings cut in the upper thighs. A row of these figures decorated the sides of a coffin to which they had been fixed with small nails, the inner side of the leather covered with tin foil facing outwards.

47, 48

49

**49 Tiger savaging an elk –
appliqué decoration from a saddle**
Leather; length 34cm; width 21cm.
High Altai, Pazyryk, barrow 1. Excavations
of M. P. Gryaznov, 1929.
Early nomadic culture; 5th century BC.
Hermitage. 1295/250.
Bibliography: Rudenko, 1970. p. 230, fig. 108.

A leather appliqué decoration, portraying in
silhouette a scene of a tiger attacking an elk. The
predator has sunk his teeth and claws into the
crupper of the fleeing elk and with one paw is
gripping his prey by its rear leg. The whole
scene is imbued with movement and drama. The
theme of animals fighting occupies a dominant
place in the art of the ancient Altai and such
compositions reflect the real life of the ancient
nomads – a life of endless wars, raids, victories
and defeats. Although heavily influenced by
Near Eastern art, these subjects are enriched by
the introduction of an element of realism and
become more expressive than their Iranian
originals.

50, 51 Appliqué decorations from a saddle
Leather; lengths 16.5cm and 16.3cm;
widths 3.6cm and 3.3cm.
High Altai, Pazyryk, barrow 1. Excavations
of M. P. Gryaznov, 1929.
Early nomadic culture; 5th century BC.
Hermitage. 1295/304, 305.
Bibliography: Rudenko, 1970. p. 144, fig. 72E.

Open-work appliqué decorations from an
arched saddle-bow, with a design in the form of
pairs of volutes.

50

51

52 Stag-finial

Wood, leather; height 11.5cm; width 6cm.
High Altai, Pazyryk, barrow 2. Excavations
of S. I. Rudenko, 1947.
Early nomadic culture; 5th century BC.
Hermitage. 1684/154.
Bibliography: Rudenko, 1970. pl. 137H.

The body of this miniature sculpture of a stag is
carved with its pedestal from a single piece of
wood. The correct proportions of the body are
strictly observed but the antlers, cut from thick,
stiff leather, have been deliberately exaggerated.
The beauty of the image and the skill of
execution justify the inclusion of this figure
among the masterpieces of small-scale sculpture.

This is one of four similar figures found in
various places in the burial chamber. Their
purpose is unclear. In the bases of the globe-
shaped pedestals are small iron rods, indicating
that the figures served as finials on objects of
some kind.

52

53 Head of a deer in the beak of a gryphon

Wood, leather; length 23cm; width 16.5cm.
High Altai, Pazyryk, barrow 2. Excavations
of S. I. Rudenko, 1947.
Early nomadic culture; 5th century BC.
Hermitage. 1684/169.
Bibliography: Rudenko.
1970. pl. 142D.

53

The purpose of this splendid example of wood
carving, representing a gryphon holding a deer's
head in its beak, is not clear. The gryphon's
small head and short neck are carved from
wood, but its ears, comb and large wings
(placed beside the beak), are cut from thick
leather. The deer's antlers, also cut from leather,
are treated in an original manner, each tine
ending in a cockerel's head on a long neck.
This composition has a particular
significance as a conventional representation of the main theme in
the art of the ancient Altai –
animals fighting and the
embodiment of victory.

57

△ 54

54 Head of a fantastic bird
Wood, leather, gold; height 21.5cm; width 15cm.
High Altai, Pazyryk, barrow 3. Excavations
of S. I. Rudenko, 1948.
Early nomadic culture; 5th–4th centuries BC.
Hermitage. 1685/397.
Bibliography: Rudenko, 1970. pl. 121B.

A wooden finial sculptured in the form of a
fantastic bird's head with a zoomorphic shape on
its beak. The head originally had leather horns
and ears and was covered with gold leaf. This
image is unique amongst works of Altai art.

55 Horse's bridle
Wood, leather, gold; dimensions 51 × 43cm.
Plaques with representations of a ram 10 × 10cm;
palmette-plaques 9 × 9cm; length of bars 11cm;
frontal plaque 12 × 9cm; cheek-pieces 21cm.
High Altai, Pazyryk, barrow 1. Excavations of
M. P. Gryaznov, 1929.
Early nomadic culture; 5th century BC.
Hermitage. 1295/189.
Bibliography: Rudenko, 1970. pl. 82.

55 ▽

A typical ancient Altai bridle. It consists of three
straps: two side-straps, which become cheek-
straps at their lower ends, and a nose-strap. The
straps are decorated with nine plaques or plates:
four in the form of stylised palmettes, and five
representing the facing heads of mountain rams
complete with large, sharply-curved horns of
leather. Towards the cheek-pieces the cheek-
straps divide into two forks which are joined to
the cheek-pieces and decorated with rows of
volutes. The design of the cheek-pieces deserves
particular attention; they portray mountain
rams furiously galloping or leaping, their bodies
horizontally extended with the forelegs drawn
up and the hind legs thrown backwards. The
impression of movement is accentuated by the
absence of a surface under the ram's feet, so that
the figures seem to be soaring through the air.
The bridle has no forehead strap and its function
was performed by a narrow thong embellished
by a pear-shaped frontal plate. All the wooden
adornments of the bridle were originally
covered with gold-leaf of which only fragments
have survived.

56

56 Figure of a mountain ram
Wood, leather; length 10.4cm; width 8.9cm.
High Altai, Pazyryk, barrow 3. Excavations
of S. I. Rudenko, 1948.
Early nomadic culture; 5th–4th centuries BC.
Hermitage. 1685/151.
Bibliography: Rudenko, 1970. pl. 99C.

Harness plaque carved in relief with the figure of
a mountain ram. The unnatural twisting of the
hind quarters (a frequently used device in the
art of the ancient Altai) both makes the image
more dynamic and creates a circular composition
which corresponds to the essential form of the
object.

57, 58 Heads of elks
Wood; lengths 10cm and 10.1cm;
widths 4.2cm and 4cm.
High Altai, Pazyryk, barrow 3. Excavations
of S. I. Rudenko, 1948.
Early nomadic culture; 5th–4th centuries BC.
Hermitage. 1685/140, 142.
Bibliography: Rudenko, 1970. pl. 100B, C.

Harness decorations in the form of elks' heads in profile. The heads are skilfully modelled, with half-open mouths, almond-shaped eyes and oval grooved ears. Their original red colouring has been preserved in places but the leather horns with which they were originally equipped have since been lost. This subject is a favourite one and occurs frequently in the art of the Altai.

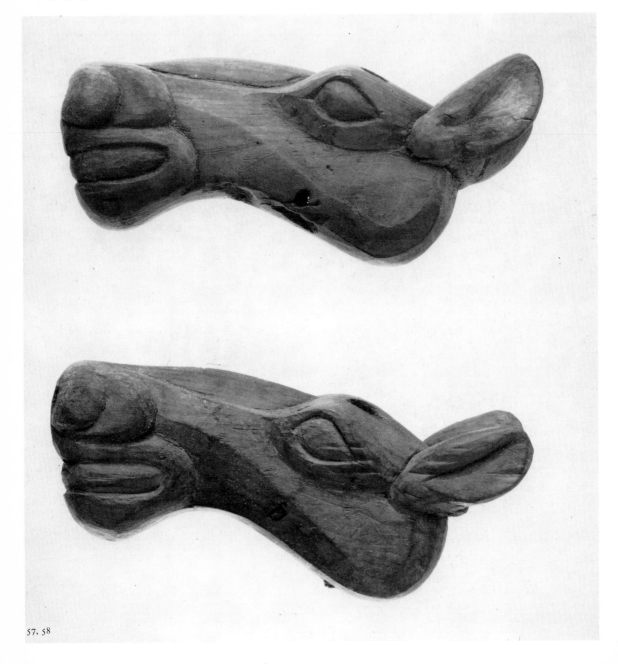

57, 58

△59, 60   61 ▽

59, 60 Saddle-bow decorations

Wood; length 16.7cm; widths 6cm and 6.2cm.
High Altai, Pazyryk, barrow 3. Excavations
of S. I. Rudenko, 1948.
Early nomadic culture; 5th–4th centuries BC.
Hermitage. 1685/198, 199.
Bibliography: Rudenko, 1970, pl. 101A.

Wooden saddle-bow embellishments in the form
of arch-shaped convex plates decorated with
a pair of symmetrical elk-heads on a red
background. The raised surfaces and rim were
covered with gold leaf. Ancient Altai saddles
differed from those now in use since they were
without wooden frames; they consisted simply
of two soft leather cushions, sewn together along
one side and stuffed with reindeer hair or,
occasionally, grass. They were held on the
horse's back with a girth-strap and steadied by
breast- and crupper-straps. The front and rear
of the saddle (the bows) were raised higher than
the seat because they were more thickly padded.
The saddle-bows were embellished with
wooden or bone plates. Stirrups or loops for the
feet were not yet used and saddle blankets (cat.
no. 37) were placed under the saddles and
elegant felt coverlets (cat. no. 36) were spread
over them.

61 Harness decoration in the form of an elk's head

Wood; height 11.2cm; width 7cm.
Central Altai, Tuekta, barrow 1. Excavations
of S. I. Rudenko, 1954.
Early nomadic culture; 6th century BC.
Hermitage. 2179/205.
Bibliography: Rudenko, 1960. pl. XCII.

Plaque carved in low relief with the head of an
elk in profile, a crest on its forehead and a comb
on its neck, the two separated by an ornamental
palmette. The body is rendered as an
ornamental volute. The plaque was fastened to a
bridle by special lugs on the reverse.

62

62 Harness decoration – plaque in low relief in the form of two elks' heads

Wood; dimensions 7 × 8.8cm.
Central Altai, Tuekta, barrow 1. Excavations
of S. I. Rudenko, 1954.
Early nomadic culture; 6th century BC.
Hermitage. 2179/227.
Bibliography: Rudenko, 1960. pl. XCI.

Carved plaque in low relief portraying two
heraldically opposed elks' heads joined by a
shared ear. This composition can be interpreted
as one head divided vertically and spread out in
one plane.

63 Harness decoration – plaque in low relief in the form of three elks' heads

Wood; 8.3 × 8.8cm.
Central Altai, Tuekta, barrow 1. Excavations
of S. I. Rudenko, 1954.
Early nomadic culture; 6th century BC.
Hermitage. 2179/245.
Bibliography: Rudenko, 1960. pl. XCI, 6.

Plaque carved in low relief with a composition
of three elks' heads arranged in a triple palmette.

64 Saddle decoration – plaque in the form of an eagle

Wood; 14.5 × 24.4cm.
Central Altai, Bash-Adar, barrow 2. Excavations
of S. I. Rudenko, 1950.
Early nomadic culture; 6th century BC.
Hermitage. 1793/347.
Bibliography: Gryaznov, 1969. p. 142.

Plaque from the front of a saddle-bow carved in
relief with the figure of an eagle. The bird is
shown facing with its head turned to its right, a
powerful beak, a large ear with a scroll in the
centre, outspread wings and strong talons. The
representation of the plumage on the broad
breast resembles a scaled coat of mail. Four such
plaques were found – two on the front saddle-
bow and two on the rear. The plaques are
curved to fit the curve of the saddle and were all
originally covered with gold leaf.

63

64

65

67

65 Harness decoration – figurine of an eagle in low relief

Wood; height 4.5cm; width 3.5cm.
Central Altai, Tuekta, barrow 1. Excavations
of S. I. Rudenko, 1954.
Early nomadic culture; 6th century BC.
Hermitage. 2179/120.
Bibliography: Rudenko, 1960. pl. XCVII.

This miniature figurine of an eagle in low relief
is an embellishment from a set of horse harness.
The bird is portrayed with its head turned to the
left and its outspread wings pointing downwards.
The plumage of the wings and tail is conveyed
by soft, flowing, incised lines. Such designs from
the Scythian period are familiar not only in the
Altai and on the Yenisei but also in the Northern
Black Sea coast area.

66 Frontal plaque

Wood; diameter 12.7cm.
Central Altai, Tuekta, barrow 1. Excavations
of S. I. Rudenko, 1954.
Early nomadic culture; 6th century BC.
Hermitage. 2179/79.
Bibliography: Rudenko, 1970. pl. 143E.

Within the circular shape of this frontal plaque
from a horse's bridle the figures of two gryphons
have been skilfully placed. The gryphons are
portrayed as fantastic birds with predatory beaks,
feral ears, manes in the form of stylized deer-
antlers and powerful wings. The details of the
figures are conveyed by skilful carving – the
folded wings by curved incised lines and the
plumage on the breasts by overlapping scales.
Its perfection of composition and skill of
execution place this object among the
masterpieces of the art of the ancient Altai.
Colour plate

67 Plaque-pendant in the form of two gryphons

Wood; height 12cm; width 9cm.
Central Altai, Tuekta, barrow 1. Excavations
of S. I. Rudenko, 1954.
Early nomadic culture; 6th century BC.
Hermitage. 2179/28.
Bibliography: Artamonov, 1973. p. 230, fig. 303.

The subject of this plaque-pendant (a decoration from a horse's bridle) was borrowed from the Near East and is a very popular motif in the art of the ancient Altai. The purely decorative aspect of this piece is emphasised by the way in which the body of the gryphon is reduced to a volute terminating in a second gryphon's head at the tip of the 'tail'.

68 Palmette-plaque
set with a sculptural gryphon's head
Wood; 6.5 × 7cm.
Central Altai, Tuekta, barrow 1. Excavations of S. I. Rudenko, 1954.
Early nomadic culture; 6th century BC.
Hermitage. 2179/96.
Bibliography: Rudenko, 1960. pl. XCLIX, 7.

This plaque, a pendant from a horse's bridle, combines a flat palmette of complex form with a sculptural gryphon's head. The head, which originally had leather ears, terminates in a peg which fits into a socket in the plaque.

69 Sculptural gryphon's head
Wood; 11 × 10cm.
Central Altai, Tuekta, barrow 1. Excavations of S. I. Rudenko, 1954.
Early nomadic culture; 6th century BC.
Hermitage. 2179/109.
Bibliography: Rudenko, 1960. pl. XCIX, 1.

Wooden head of a gryphon carved in the round (a decoration from a horse's bridle). It has a sharply curved beak, a jutting crest, a mane and upright ears. The head was apparently glued to a plate of wood, leather or bronze, but this has not survived.

70 Anthropomorphic plaque
Wood; 11 × 10cm.
High Altai, Pazyryk, barrow 1. Excavations of M. P. Gryaznov, 1929.
Early nomadic culture; 5th century BC.
Hermitage. 1295/392.
Bibliography: Rudenko, 1970. pl. 92A.

This bridle-plaque bears a representation in relief of a human face – an extremely rare motif in the art of the ancient Altai. The face is flat

△68

69 ▽

△71

72▽

with high cheekbones, has a low brow, a high narrow nose and thin lips emphasising the slitted mouth. The semi-circular ears are set high on the side of the head and the hair and beard which frame the face are indicated by incised grooves. Rudenko has compared this piece with the bearded face with a Gorgon's protruding tongue on a round gold plaque in the Oxus Treasure (in the British Museum, no. 32), and with a representation of a bearded face on a bronze dish from Ziwiye.
Colour plate

71, 72 Sculptural figurines of tigers

Wood; length of base 8.5cm; widths 5.9cm and 5.7cm; length of figures 6.2cm and 7cm.
High Altai, Pazyryk, barrow 2. Excavations of S. I. Rudenko, 1947.
Early nomadic culture; 5th century BC.
Hermitage. 1684/367, 368.
Bibliography: Rudenko, 1970. pl. 93A.

These red-coloured sculptural figurines of tigers (decorations from a horse's bridle) are mounted on wooden bases with rounded fore-edges. The animals are shown half-reclining on their sides with their legs drawn up, their forelegs extended and their ears attentively raised. Each figure is fastened to its base by a narrow thong which also attached the plaque to the bridle.

73, 74 Sculptural figurines of tiger cubs

Wood; lengths 4.8cm and 4.7cm; maximum height 2.8cm.
High Altai, Pazyryk, barrow 3. Excavations of S. I. Rudenko, 1948.
Early nomadic culture; 5th–4th centuries BC.
Hermitage. 1685/187, 188.
Bibliography: Rudenko, 1970. pl. 102E.

These figurines of tiger cubs were used to decorate the bow of a saddle. The animals are portrayed with thick muzzles, half open mouths with soft creases over the upper lip, and round eyes and ears with scrolls in the centre. The miniature bodies terminate in pertly raised tails. These and their fellows were sewn to the edge of the saddle-bow in profile. They were alternately either coloured red or covered with gold leaf.

△73   74▽

75

75 Plaque in the form of a tiger's face
Bone; length 8cm; width 8.8cm.
Altai. Chance find. Frolov Collection.
Early nomadic culture; 5th–3rd centuries BC.
Hermitage. 1122/1.
Bibliography: Rudenko, 1970. pl. 138D.

Saddle pendant in the form of a bone plaque
with a carved representation of a tiger's face.
The animal has erect leaf-shaped ears with a
scroll at their base, elongated eyes, flaring
nostrils and a wrinkled upper lip. The teeth are
framed by a large upcurved mouth and the
characteristically feline cheeks curve down to
terminate in volutes. The whole range of
techniques characteristic of the Scytho-Siberian
animal style is present. The red paint with which
the whole head was originally covered can still
be seen in places. The pendant was attached to
the saddle by the round hole in its upper part.

76

76 Plaque representing a tiger
Wood; length 10.3cm; height 6.8cm.
Altai. Chance find. Frolov Collection.
Early nomadic culture; 5th–3rd centuries BC.
Hermitage. 1122/8.
Bibliography: Rudenko, 1970. pl. 138B.

This wooden plaque (a decoration from a horse's
harness) portrays a tiger's head in profile with
its ear laid back to its head, a snarling mouth and
a large volute on the lower jaw. Between the
ear and the volute is a small round hole through
which the plaque was fastened to the harness-
strap.

77

77 Plaque representing a tiger
Wood; length 8cm; width 4.4cm.
Altai. Chance find. Frolov Collection.
Early nomadic culture; 5th–3rd centuries BC.
Hermitage. 1122/9.
Bibliography: Rudenko, 1970. pl. 138E.

This decoration from a horse's harness portrays a
tiger's head carved in low relief. The head with
its snarling mouth is shown in left profile. In
place of the neck is a small cylindrical shaft
which was probably originally inserted into a
flat base.

78 Cheek-piece

Wood; length 18cm; width 4cm.
High Altai, Pazyryk, barrow 3. Excavations
of S. I. Rudenko, 1948.
Early nomadic culture; 6th–5th centuries BC.
Hermitage. 1685/109.
Bibliography: Rudenko, 1970. pl. 104A.

This wooden cheek-piece is typical of those
found on ancient Altai bridles. It is curved in the
form of a letter 'S' and embellished on the upper
end with the head of a fantastic tiger in profile
and on the lower with the head of a gryphon.
The tiger has open jaws framing jutting fangs, a
wrinkled upper lip, a large elongated eye, a long
ear with a scroll at its base and a short,
segmented horn. The gryphon is represented in a
very conventional manner, the head being no
more than a highly expressive sketch. This
method of representing gryphons' heads is
known not only in the Altai but also in the art
of the Scythians of the steppes north of the
Black Sea.
Colour plate

79 Detail of horse's harness embellished with plaques representing a tiger and a trefoil

Wood, leather, bronze; length 22.5cm; height of
wooden plaque 12.5cm.
Central Altai, Tuekta, barrow 1. Excavations
of S. I. Rudenko, 1954.
Early nomadic culture; 6th century BC.
Hermitage. 2179/148.
Bibliography: Gryaznov, 1969. pl. 157.

Facing head of a tiger with its greedy, fanged
mouth stretching the whole width of the muzzle
and its ears jutting upwards from a scrolled base.
The body is represented conventionally as a
trefoil palmette, the two outer leaves of which
have been transmuted into symmetrical, stylised
gryphons' heads whose bodies, in the form of
two volutes, frame the third leaf. The decoration
of the harness consists of alternate wooden and
bronze trefoil-shaped plaques.

80 Sculptural head of a tiger – decoration of a horse's harness

Wood; 3.3 × 4.5cm.
Central Altai, Tuekta, barrow 1. Excavations
of S. I. Rudenko, 1954.
Early nomadic culture; 6th century BC.
Hermitage. 2179/187.
Bibliography: Rudenko, 1960. pl. CII.

Tiger's head sculpted in the round.
Characteristically, the beast is portrayed with
snarling fangs. The round eye, raised upper lip,
long blunt muzzle and semi-circular ear make
this head a masterly example of wood carving.
The head merges into a graceful neck which
terminates with a peg by which it could be set
into a flat wooden or bronze figure.

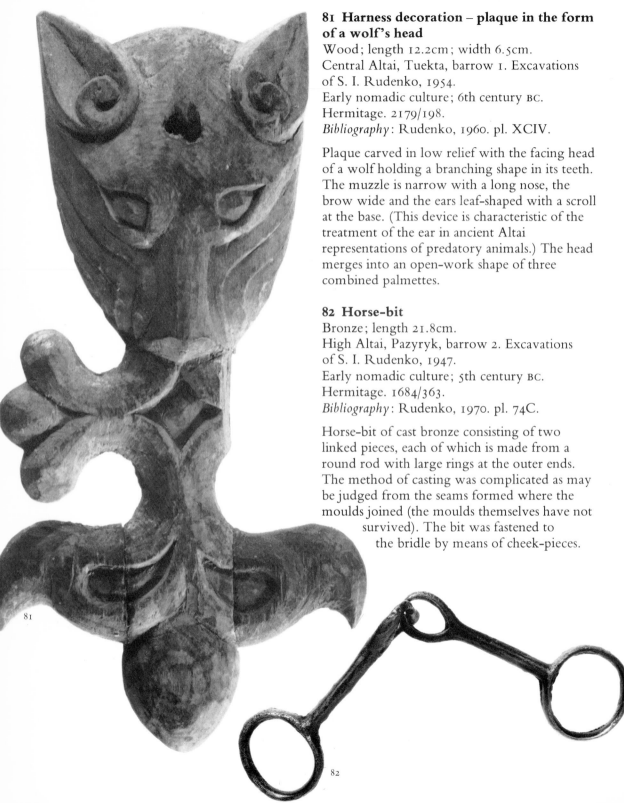

81 Harness decoration – plaque in the form of a wolf's head

Wood; length 12.2cm; width 6.5cm.
Central Altai, Tuekta, barrow 1. Excavations of S. I. Rudenko, 1954.
Early nomadic culture; 6th century BC.
Hermitage. 2179/198.
Bibliography: Rudenko, 1960. pl. XCIV.

Plaque carved in low relief with the facing head of a wolf holding a branching shape in its teeth. The muzzle is narrow with a long nose, the brow wide and the ears leaf-shaped with a scroll at the base. (This device is characteristic of the treatment of the ear in ancient Altai representations of predatory animals.) The head merges into an open-work shape of three combined palmettes.

82 Horse-bit

Bronze; length 21.8cm.
High Altai, Pazyryk, barrow 2. Excavations of S. I. Rudenko, 1947.
Early nomadic culture; 5th century BC.
Hermitage. 1684/363.
Bibliography: Rudenko, 1970. pl. 74C.

Horse-bit of cast bronze consisting of two linked pieces, each of which is made from a round rod with large rings at the outer ends. The method of casting was complicated as may be judged from the seams formed where the moulds joined (the moulds themselves have not survived). The bit was fastened to the bridle by means of cheek-pieces.

83, 84 Cheek-pieces
Wood, gold; lengths 19cm and 17.5cm.
High Altai, Pazyryk, barrow 2. Excavations
of S. I. Rudenko, 1947.
Early nomadic culture; 5th century BC.
Hermitage. 1684/364, 365.
Bibliography: Rudenko, 1970. pl. 93C.

S-shaped cheek-pieces embellished at the ends
with carvings in relief of half-figures of tigers in
profile. The animals are portrayed with open
jaws, the characteristic wrinkles on the upper lip,
and the fore-paw touches the lower jaw. Detail
on the sharp standing-up ears and the ruff is
conveyed by ridged grooves. The cheek-pieces
were covered with gold leaf, some of which
has been preserved.

   These cheek-pieces come from the same bridle
as the bits (no. 82) and the plaques (nos. 76, 77).

85 Horse-bit
Iron; length 20cm; diameter 3cm.
High Altai, Pazyryk, barrow 2. Excavations
of S. I. Rudenko, 1947.
Early nomadic culture; 5th century BC.
Hermitage. 1684/429.
Bibliography: Rudenko, 1970. pl. 74C.

Forged iron horse-bit, consisting of two linked
pieces with elongated rings at the ends.

86 Bridle-decoration – *saiga* **antelope's head**
Wood; length 6.5cm; height of head 3.2cm.
High Altai, Pazyryk, barrow 5. Excavations
of S. I. Rudenko, 1949.
Early nomadic culture; 5th–4th centuries BC.
Hermitage. 1687/158.
Bibliography: Rudenko, 1970. pl. 115A.

Bridle-decoration in the form of a carved head
of a *saiga* antelope. The long, hooked, blunt
nose, round eye and spiral horns are
characteristic of this animal. The
mouth is slightly open and the
lower jaw terminates in a
scroll. Representations of
saiga antelopes in ancient
Altai art are rare but
very expressive.

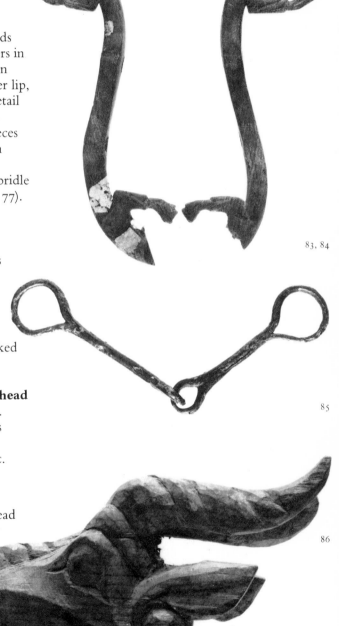

83, 84

85

86

71

87

87 Bridle-decoration – head of a tiger
Wood, leather, lacquer; length of leather base
7cm; width 4cm; length of head 4cm; height 3cm.
High Altai, Pazyryk, barrow 5. Excavations
of S. I. Rudenko, 1949.
Early nomadic culture; 5th–4th centuries BC.
Hermitage. 1687/150.
Bibliography: Rudenko, 1970. pl. 117B.

This sculptural head of a tiger (a bridle-
decoration) exhibits the usual stylistic devices:
the wrinkles on the upper lip, the elongated eye
and the scroll at the base of the ear. The head is
attached to a flat leaf-shaped leather base
covered with red lacquer.

88, 89 Saddle-pendants
Wood; lengths 9cm and 8.5cm; widths 8cm
and 7.5cm.
High Altai, Pazyryk, barrow 5. Excavations
of S. I. Rudenko, 1949.
Early nomadic culture; 5th–4th centuries BC.
Hermitage. 1687/208, 209.
Bibliography: Rudenko, 1970. pl. 116E.

These shield-shaped saddle-pendants, originally
attached to the ends of the straps joining the two
saddle-cushions, are decorated with stylised
facing tigers' heads. The heads have narrow
noses, large slanting eyes, and large curved
mouths with wrinkled upper lips. The flat upper
edges of the plaques each have three small holes
through which leather thongs were threaded.

90, 91 Decorative plaques from a bridle
Wood; 6.5 × 6.5cm, and 7 × 6.5cm.
High Altai, Pazyryk, barrow 4. Excavations
of S. I. Rudenko, 1948.
Early nomadic culture; 5th–4th centuries BC.
Hermitage. 1686/31, 32.
Bibliography: Rudenko, 1970. pl. 110B.

Plaques (bridle-decorations) representing wolves
with violently curved bodies and their fore- and
hind-quarters twisted in opposite directions.
This method of conveying violent movement is
very characteristic of the ancient art of the Altai
and Siberia.

   The disproportionately large heads of the
wolves are turned backwards. The long narrow

88

90

nose, the eye carved in relief, the open mouth with wrinkled upper lip showing the fangs, as if the animal were gnashing its teeth – all these devices, in spite of their conventional nature, convey the predatory nature of the beast with striking fidelity.

The plaques were attached to the bridle-straps by loops on the reverse.

92, 93 Decorative plaques from a bridle
Wood; 9.8 × 5cm, and 9.5 × 5.5cm.
High Altai, Pazyryk, barrow 4. Excavations of S. I. Rudenko, 1948.
Early nomadic culture; 5th–4th centuries BC.
Hermitage. 1686/51, 52.
Bibliography: Rudenko, 1970. pl. 110F.

Bridle-plaques in the form of wolves' heads with open jaws holding roebucks' heads. The muzzles of the wolves are long and narrow with elongated eyes and leaf-shaped ears; their upper lips are wrinkled and the lower jaws terminate in a scroll. The roebucks' heads are particularly expressive with elongated ears and diamond-shaped eyes having round, protruding pupils.

The roebucks' heads and the lower jaws and ears of the wolves were painted red. The remaining surface of the plaques was covered with gold leaf.

Such symbolic representations of fighting animals were very popular in the art of the ancient Altai.
Colour plate

94, 95 Decorative strap-facings from horse's harness

Wood; 11.2 × 3.5cm, and 11.3 × 3.7cm.
High Altai, Pazyryk, barrow 3. Excavations
of S. I. Rudenko, 1948.
Early nomadic culture; 5th–4th centuries BC.
Hermitage. 1685/248, 249.
Bibliography: Rudenko, 1970. pl. 102I, J.

These two elongated trapezoidal plates, carved
with the figures of hares, were used to embellish
the crupper-straps near the rear saddle-bow. The
animals are portrayed with round, softly
outlined muzzles, large elongated ears parallel to
the body and powerful paws which, on one
plaque have two claws and on the other, three.
The fore-quarters are stretched sharply forward,
as if the animal were running; the hind-quarters
are twisted through 180 degrees – a stylistic
device characteristically used in ancient Altai art
to indicate violent movement or, possibly, to
suggest that the animal is wounded. The figures
are accommodated in the wider ends of the
plates; in the narrow ends are tooth-like shapes –
three on one plaque and four on the other.
Rudenko is of the opinion that the 'teeth' are a
conventional method of suggesting grass or
bushes. These plaques contain the only known
representations of hares in the art of the ancient
Altai. They are much more frequently found in
the art of the north coast area of the Black Sea.

The frames of the plaques and the figures of
the hares were originally covered with gold leaf
and the background painted red.

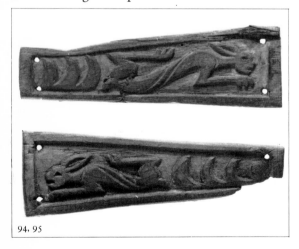

94, 95

96, 97 Saddle pendants

Wood; 9 × 9cm, and 8.5 × 7cm.
High Altai, Pazyryk, barrow 3. Excavations
of S. I. Rudenko, 1948.
Early nomadic culture; 5th–4th centuries BC.
Hermitage. 1685/225, 232.
Bibliography: Rudenko, 1970. pl. 102B.

Shield-shaped saddle-strap embellishments
covered with a relief design of stylised deer-
antlers. In his desire to fit the ornament into the
shape of the object while decorating the whole
available surface, the craftsman has added to and
complicated the motif of the basic design.

The holes by which the pendant was fastened
to the strap can be seen along the straight upper
edge. The border of the plaque and the design
were covered with gold leaf and the background
was coloured red.

Colour plate

97

98, 99 Palmette-plaques from a horse's harness

Wood; lengths 9.5cm.
High Altai, Pazyryk, barrow 1. Excavations
of M. P. Gryaznov, 1929.
Early nomadic culture; 5th century BC.
Hermitage. 1295/217, 219.
Bibliography: Rudenko, 1970. pl. 79A.

Pendant-plaques from horse harness in the form
of elegant palmettes consisting of three petals in
the shape of a fan cupped in spirally curving
leaves. This is a local variant of the lotus flower
motif which came to the Altai from the art of
the Near East.

98

100

100 Bridle

Wood, leather; 45 × 37cm; diameter of plaques
6.4cm; length of cheek-pieces 18.5cm.
High Altai, Pazyryk, barrow 5. Excavations
of S. I. Rudenko, 1949.
Early nomadic culture; 5th–4th centuries BC.
Hermitage. 1687/116.
Bibliography: Rudenko, 1970. pl. 114.

Horse's bridle of doubled leather straps. The
edges of the straps were turned inwards and
sewn together with twisted sinew threads, after
which the seam was smoothed flat. The result
was a strap with one smooth side and one with a
longitudinal seam. Fastened to the points where
the straps cross and in the middle of the nose-
strap there are seven disc-shaped plaques, each
with two concentric ridges round the rim and a
hemispherical boss in the centre. The frontal
plaque and the ends of the straight cheek-pieces
are of the same form. The plaques on the ends of
the cheek-pieces are larger than the rings on the

bit; the upper plaque was cut off and glued back
in place after the cheek-pieces had been inserted
in the rings. Each cheek-piece is pierced by two
holes through which pass the divided ends of the
side straps which are covered by wooden forks
with a 'running-wave' decoration.

101 Plate in the form of a reclining horse

Bone; length 11cm.
Tomb of Sagla-Bazha II in Western Tuva.
Excavations of A. D. Grach, 1961.
Early nomadic culture; 5th–3rd centuries BC.
Hermitage. 2351/268.
Bibliography: Artamonov, 1973. p. 81, fig. 105.

A bone plate in the form of a reclining horse,
its legs drawn up and its head slightly bowed.
The mane is indicated by a row of curved, leaf-
shaped cells of a kind which in metal objects are
usually embellished with coloured inlays. The
incised ornament decorating the whole figure
forms vortices on the shoulder and haunch

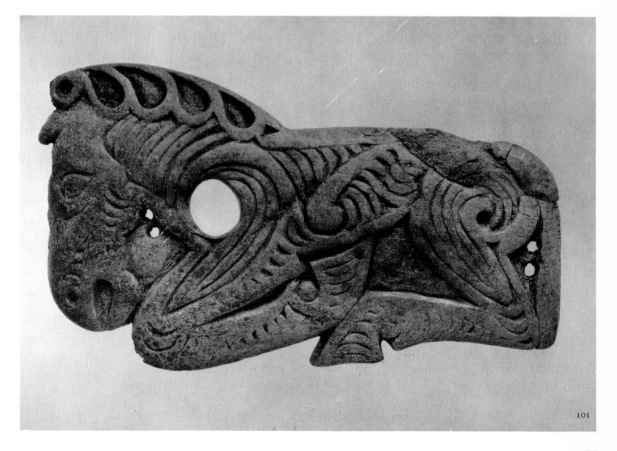

101

accentuating the muscular structure. The plate
was attached through four small holes (two by
the neck and two by the tail), and the large hole
probably had a functional purpose.

In subject, composition and style of carving
this creation of an ancient Tuvan craftsman is
close to the Altai animal style.

102 Mirror

Bronze; diameter 6.2cm.
Tomb of Sagla-Bazha II in Western Tuva.
Excavations of A. D. Grach, 1961.
Early nomadic culture; 5th–3rd centuries BC.
Hermitage. 2351/286.
Bibliography: Artamonov, 1973. p. 81, fig. 104.

A bronze mirror with a loop-shaped handle. On
the handle is a scene of fighting animals in which
a predator, standing in profile, is biting the head
of a goat. The composition is balanced on one
side by the predator's raised tail with a curled
tip, and on the other by the goat's horn. A
second predator is represented only by its facing
head, placed on the back of the first.

On the haunch and shoulder of the predator
are leaf-shaped settings for coloured inlays.
Overall, and in the treatment of some details,
this object is close to certain articles in the
Siberian Collection of Peter the Great.

102

THE TAGAR CULTURE

Catalogue numbers 103–127

The Minusinsk basin, which is surrounded on three sides by mountains and on the north by *taiga* (coniferous forest), was inhabited from the seventh to the third centuries BC by tribes named after the Tagar lake and island near Minusinsk. These peoples built very distinctive barrows whose stone walls have large pillars at the corners and at intervals along the sides. These unusual megalithic constructions are found everywhere – on the steppe, along river valleys and on mountain slopes – and they have become an integral part of the surrounding landscape.

The curious appearance of the barrows and the vast numbers of bronze artefacts from this area have long attracted attention. Already by the eighteenth century the local population had acquired a considerable store of bronzes discovered whilst ploughing, or plundered from barrows; as a result Soviet and other museums throughout the world, have amassed tens of thousands of bronze antiquities. The most important collection in the Hermitage, made by a mining engineer, I. A. Lopatin, during the second half of the nineteenth century, consists of two thousand objects.

Archaeological expeditions are another important source for museum collections. The first expedition to Siberia, sent by Peter the Great for research in the natural sciences, was engaged in both ethnographical and archaeological work. In 1722 its Director, D. G. Messerschmidt, carried out the first excavation of a Tagar barrow, near the town of Krasnoturansk on the right bank of the Yenisei. Unfortunately the archaeological material he found is known only from eighteenth-century drawings preserved in the *Kunstkammer*. In 1725, following the foundation of the Russian Academy of Sciences, Siberia began to be explored by expeditions with a wide range of interests. The historian G. F. Miller, while on the staff of the Kamchatka Expedition of 1733–43, acquired in Krasnoyarsk a collection of bronze finials decorated with animal-style figures characteristic of the Minusinsk basin (cat. no. 104). The excavations of V. V. Radlov in 1863 and also of A. V. Adrianov at the turn of the century still further enriched the Hermitage with valuable collections from the Tagar culture. During the 1920s S. A. Teploukhov and S. V. Kiselev began the systematic investigation of the area, and thirty years later large-scale archaeological expeditions to Siberia were mounted by the Institute of Archaeology of the Academy of Sciences of the USSR. Soviet laws provide for the allocation of substantial funds to excavate and study archaeological monuments faced with destruction, and under these provisions the Krasnoyarsk Expedition (1958–71), directed by M. P. Gryaznov, recorded sites due to be flooded in the construction of the Krasnoyarsk Hydro-electric Station. All the material collected by this expedition has been acquired by the Hermitage.

Unlike the nomadic tribes the Tagar population practised agriculture, aided by irrigation, as well as herding. They cultivated millet and kept cows and sheep. Horses are not found in the burials, but their importance can be judged from finds of bronze bits, cheek-pieces and harness-mounts.

Burials were in stone cists or chambers surrounded by walls of stone slabs with taller stones at the corners and at intervals along the sides. Weapons, such as daggers, axes and quivers of arrows, were placed in men's graves whilst the graves of women contained knives, awls, mirrors and ornaments. Burials of both sexes were provided with pottery vessels containing drink and lavishly supplied with select cuts and joints of mutton and beef. Usually there was only the one body in each grave, but from the fifth century BC small family graves (husband, wife and child) begin to appear, and even collective tombs with a hundred or more burials.

A hierarchical society based on property ownership and differences in social position is attested by some imposing barrows, up to ten metres in height and 500 metres in circumference, which are found alongside the small and medium-size mounds. In one such barrow – the Royal Barrow at Salbyk, excavated by S. V. Kiselev in 1954–56 – the twenty stone slabs at the corners and along the sides were up to five metres high and weighed thirty to forty tons each.

Rich deposits of ore led to the Minusinsk basin becoming an important centre of ancient metal-working. As well as making single objects in simple moulds the local smiths also tackled more complex problems of casting in order to produce bronze cauldrons and other works of art.

The images and ideas of the Tagar tribes are embodied in their art, where the central figures are the mountain goat and birds of prey. They also portrayed boars, bears, wolves and tigers, but representations of horses, wild asses, deer, fish and *saiga* antelope are rare. Figures of animals modelled in the round, usually standing and cast in metal, were used to decorate knives, battle-axes, daggers, tools and details of horse-harness.

Bronze plaques showing deer with their legs tucked up and their antlers cast back along the spine make their appearance in Tagar art in the fifth century BC. This subject, which was a particular favourite with the Scythians, achieved widespread popularity and was most successfully adapted locally in the Minusinsk region.

The art of the Tagar culture is characterised by a localised form of stylization, with animals represented in quiescent attitudes; there is little in the way of dynamic action. Scenes of battling animals and fantastic beasts are absent – although there is a plaque showing a tiger with the head of a mountain ram in its jaws. Tagar plastic art lacks almost any further embellishment, so its forms are spare but full of expression whilst the artists were superb at naturalistic renderings of their animal subjects. Unfortunately we know nothing of their work in organic materials.

Another series of decorated bronzes illustrates a different form of stylization common to Southern Siberia and Central Asia (see, for example, cat. nos. 108 and 120).

103 Handle of a cauldron

Copper; height 11.4cm.
Chadobets Village. Krasnoyarsk Region.
Chance find. Collection of I. A. Lopatin,
nineteenth century.
Tagar culture; 7th century BC.
Hermitage. 5531/1482.
Unpublished.

Cauldron handle cast in one piece in a two-part
mould in the form of a figure of a mountain
goat in the round. The legs and body are
functionally simplified but the curve of the neck
is indicated. The small head with its oval ears is
stepped forward on the neck and is almost
without details, the mouth and eyes can barely
be traced. The horn descends to reach the
animal's back.

In style this representation of a goat is
distinguished by its archaic quality and is
connected with the Late Bronze Age culture of
Southern Siberia. Handles of ritual cauldrons
in animal shapes are extremely rare in the
Khakass-Minusinsk basin.

104 Finial

Bronze; height 15.7cm.
Krasnoyarsk Region. Chance find. Collection
of G. F. Miller, 1735.
Tagar culture; 7th–6th centuries BC.
Hermitage. 1121/9.
Bibliography: Zavitukhina, 1978. p. 38.

Figure cast in bronze of a mountain goat
standing on a bell-shaped base. Both the figure
and base are hollow, the core of the mould
having been melted out through the holes in the
goat's body.

The animal's stance, with its feet placed close
together, is characteristic of the mountain goat
and the style is simple and monumental, typical
of Tagar art. Large masses are used to convey
the articulation of the body. The shoulder is
shown as a segment, and the body swells
gradually into the rounded haunch but there is
no separation between the left and right legs.
The head is elongated and flows smoothly
into the massive neck while the horns curve
down to touch the spine, the design on them

△ 103   104 ▽

indicating the annual growth-rings. The ears are upright and the nostrils and eyes are small, round cavities.

Such finials were used to cap the wooden uprights of burial couches and had a ritual significance.

105 Knife

Bronze; length 22.4cm.
Lower Abakan river. Chance find
by V. V. Radlov in 1863.
Tagar culture; 7th–6th centuries BC.
Hermitage. 1123/21.
Bibliography: Borovka, 1928. pl. 39D.

Bronze knife, cast in a two-part mould, with the figure of a mountain goat in a ring on the end of the hilt. The goat is flattened and portrayed in a manner typical of Minusinsk art. The hilt is decorated on both sides with a relief design of slanting lines and conventionalised horseshoe shapes normally used on knives, daggers and plaques.

The knife is an imitation of the composite knives which were widely distributed in the Minusinsk basin, with hollow hilts each containing an awl terminating in a ring or an animal figure.

106 Standard

Bronze; height 11.5cm; diameter 9cm.
Siberia. Origin unknown.
Tagar culture; 5th–4th centuries BC.
Hermitage. 1124/11.
Unpublished.

Bronze standard-finial cast in a two-part mould. Its upper rim is embellished with three figurines of mountain goats. The slightly flattened figures of the animals, their decorative function emphasised by their simplified, geometrical shapes, are portrayed in the traditional manner, standing on the tips of their hooves. Their heads are large with hooked muzzles and eyes are indicated by perforations. The horns, on which the annual growth-rings are shown in relief, curve sharply down to touch the neck. The fore and rear pairs of legs are not separated and the joints and hooves are exaggerated.

105

106

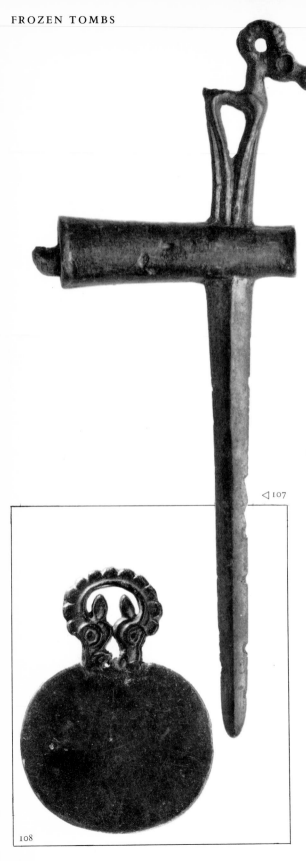

◁ 107

108

The function of such standards, which are usually found in graves together with finials (no. 104), is unknown. They were probably either placed on the tips of chieftains' battle standards or used to hold ritual torches.

107 Battle-axe

Bronze, wood; length 17.2cm.
Barrow near Mt. Barsuchikha, Krasnoyarsk Region. Excavations of M. N. Pshenitsyna, 1970.
Tagar culture; 5th–4th centuries BC.
Hermitage. 2622/48.
Unpublished.

On the butt of the axe is an elegant figure of a mountain goat in the round. The body is short and slim with raised hind quarters, its long legs rendered as decorative strips. On the graceful head the annual growth-rings can be seen on the sharply curved horns. Round cavities indicate the nostrils and the large eyes.

The southern Siberian tribes used such axes as weapons. Originally they were large and massive but by the third century BC they were losing their practical significance and acquiring a ritual function.

108 Mirror

Bronze; diameter 8cm; length of handle 3.8cm.
Village of Borodino, Krasnoyarsk Region.
Chance find. Collection of I. A. Lopatin, nineteenth century.
Tagar culture; 6th–5th centuries BC.
Hermitage. 5531/1539.
Bibliography: Scythian . . . Art, 1969. no. 68.

Disc-shaped mirrors were objects of everyday use among the Minusinsk tribes but this example is unique. Its handle is a one-sided open-work relief of a pair of heads of mountain goats joined by a shared horn, their muzzles side by side. The relief is executed in a realistic style. Along the outer edge of the horn are eleven annual growth-rings. The inner edge is framed by a narrow ridge which goes on to outline the elongated ears, the protruding pupils of the eyes, half-open mouths and the lower jaws of the heads.

The object is the work of a Minusinsk craftsman but the decoration is in the Altai style.

109 Dagger

Bronze; length 26cm; width of cross-piece 5.7cm.
Found by chance north of Minusinsk.
Collection of V. V. Radlov, 1863.
Tagar culture; 6th century BC.
Hermitage. 1123/56.
Bibliography: Ancient Siberia. p. 78.

Dagger with a pommel in the form of two
gryphons' heads in the round, facing each other
and joined at the neck. Each head has two
rounded ears and the beaks, with the patch of
bare skin at the base, are massive. On the cross-
piece are two identical mirror-images of stylised
inverted figures of wolves, muzzle to muzzle,
in a creeping position, their tails between their
legs. The dagger was cast in one piece in a two-
part mould.

110 Dagger

Iron; length 29.5cm; width of cross-piece 6.2cm.
Environs of Krasnoyarsk. Chance find.
Collection of I. A. Lopatin, nineteenth century.
Tagar culture; 5th century BC.
Hermitage. 5531/340.
Bibliography: Borovka, 1928. pl. 40C.

Dagger with double-edged blade, the pommel
embellished with a pair of gryphons' heads in
the round (see no. 109). The ears are represented
as spiral scrolls, the drop-shaped eyes are
executed in shallow relief and the brow merges
into the massive growth over the beak. The
powerful beaks are curved so that the lower
beak meets itself in a circle, creating a round
opening in the composition. The fantastic birds
executed in relief on the cross-piece are
portrayed in the same manner. Both sides of the
cross-piece, which was cast in one piece with the
hilt and blade, bear identical mirror images. The
groove on the hilt is decorated with three
S-shaped scrolls.

109

110

△111

112▽

111 Plaque

Bronze; length 9cm.
Barrow near Mt. Barsuchikha, Krasnoyarsk
Region. Excavations of M. P. Zavitukhina, 1967.
Tagar culture; 5th–4th centuries BC.
Hermitage. 2456/1.
Bibliography: Zavitukhina, 1973. fig. 7.

Plaque executed in shallow relief in the form of
a deer with a slim extended body and a short
tail. Its legs are drawn up and bent so that the
hooves meet. The neck is stretched forward, the
head slightly raised and the comb-shaped
antlers with their four points are curved parallel
to the neck and touch the shoulder-blade. The
long, narrow ear is grooved, the eye indicated
by a cavity and the mouth by a groove.
Another groove runs down the front edge of the
neck. The shoulder-blade has a wing shape.

    The reverse side is flat, and the plaque was
intended to be attached by sewing onto another
object.

112 Plaque

Bronze; length 7.5cm; width 3.8cm.
Found by chance north of Minusinsk.
Collection of V. V. Radlov, 1863.
Tagar culture; 6th–5th centuries BC.
Hermitage. 1123/74.
Bibliography: Borovka, 1928. pl. 431.

Figure in high relief of a reclining deer facing
right. On the concave reverse side are the
remains of a loop for a strap.

    The massive head with its straight nose is set
in a slightly raised attitude on a short
outstretched neck. Exaggerated antlers with four
S-shaped tines extend the whole length of the
body and the front tine curves up over the
forehead whilst the sharp, indented ear touches
the antlers. The protruding eye is surrounded by
a ridge; the mouth is indicated by a groove and
the nostril by an indentation. The treatment of
the body and folded legs is both realistic and
conventional with the front and rear legs, one
resting on the other, forming a loop.

    This is an early example, and the most
expressive, of the Minusinsk deer-plaques.

113 Knife

Bronze; length 19.8cm.
Barrow by Lake Podgornoe,
Krasnoyarsk Region.
Excavations of S. A. Teploukhov, 1930.
Tagar culture; 7th–6th centuries BC.
Hermitage. 5138/20.
Bibliography: Ancient Siberia. p. 76.

The hilt of this knife is embellished with
a figure of an elk in the round. The oval
space framed by the legs served to
suspend the knife when not in use. The
elk is portrayed in a characteristic pose,
standing on the points of its hooves. It
has a large head with a massive brow
and a pendulous muzzle. The pupils of
the eyes are represented as oval cavities
outlined by ridges and the ears are
rounded and separate. The neck is
flattened and short and the body is also
shortened whilst the shoulder-blades are
indicated by triangular shapes and the
haunch is round and convex. The
articulation of the legs, executed in
relief, is anatomically correct and
although the figure is realistic, it shows
stylistic devices characteristic of the early
Tagar art of this region.

113

114 Knife

Bronze; length 17.5cm; width 2.4cm.
Village of Ust'Abakanskoe, Krasnoyarsk Region.
Chance find. Collection of I. A. Lopatin, end of
the nineteenth century.
Tagar culture; 7th–6th centuries BC.
Hermitage. 5531/976.
Bibliography: Artamonov, 1973. no. 138.

The hilt of the knife is embellished by a highly
conventionalised figure in the round of a
reclining predatory animal. Its head is lowered,
the eye indicated by an indentation and the
mouth by a groove. The body is lean and
muscular and the legs, which are drawn up to
the body, terminate in circles. Under the figure
is an ornament of triangular scallops.

On the obverse side of the hilt is a composition
which is characteristic of Southern Siberian art:
four figures of deer, executed as silhouettes in
relief, standing on the points of their hooves,
one on top of another. Their upraised heads
have spreading antlers with four tines.

115 Dagger

Bronze; length 21.8cm.
Krasnoyarsk Region. Chance find. Collection
of A. A. Bobrinskoy.
Tagar culture; 7th century BC.
Hermitage. 5544/23.
Bibliography: Dawn of Art. no. 66.

The pommel of the hilt is a figure in the round
of a wild ass with a lowered, almost square head.
On the neck a short mane, embellished with
incised lines, is clearly indicated. The mouth and
nostrils are chased with the eyes indicated by
open spaces surrounded by ridges. The ears are
short and rounded, the abdomen sunken, and
the points of the almost triangular shoulder-
blades meet on the withers. The legs are
executed in relief in a conventional style.

Two elks' heads in the round grow gradually
into relief out of the hilt to form the crosspiece.
Their long, sharp ears are also executed in relief,
their eyes are openings surrounded by ridges.

The early date of this dagger is indicated by
the combination of stylization with a realistic
representation of the parts of the body.

114

115

116 Finial

Bone; height 6cm.
Barrow on Lake Kyzyl-Kul', Krasnoyarsk Region.
Excavations of A. V. Adrianov, 1895.
Tagar culture; 6th–5th centuries BC.
Hermitage. 1126/145.
Bibliography: Gryaznov, 1969. pl. 40.

This finial, finely carved from bone in the
form of the head and neck of a horse in the
round, is distinguished by its expressiveness and
realism. Only the flaring nostrils and the large
eyes (which are not outlined) are exaggerated.
The cheeks and the lower jaw with its pendulous
lip are emphasised and the mouth is indicated by
a slit. Deep holes mark the nostrils, the corners
of the mouth and the small, vertical ears. The
modelling of the neck is realistic and in place of
a mane runs a groove ending between the ears in
a hole which pierces the head. Pierced on both
sides by oval holes, the neck is hollow and
served as a socket. It was probably mounted on a
staff of office, but its precise function is unknown.
    The head has been highly polished by
prolonged use.

△116

117 Plaque

Bone; 2.5 × 2.7cm.
Kichik-Kyuzyur, barrow 1. Krasnoyarsk Region.
Excavations of M. P. Zavitukhina, 1965.
Tagar culture; 7th–6th centuries BC.
Hermitage. 2452/30.
Bibliography: Devlet, 1969. p. 42, fig. 5.

Plaque in the form of two symmetrical animal
heads in relief. The space in the centre had a
functional purpose and the plaque was used as a
belt-slide. The muzzles of the heads point
downwards and are joined by a common neck
in the upper frame of the central space. The eyes
and ears, placed side by side, are suggested by
round indentations outlined by ridges. The
mouths are notches in the ends of the muzzles,
themselves separated by a notch. The rib-shaped
ridges are probably intended to suggest boars'
tusks.

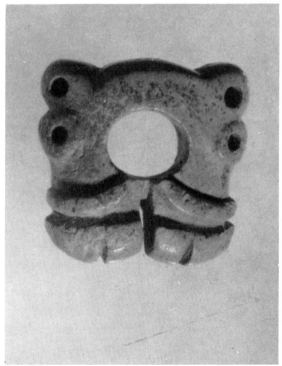

117▽

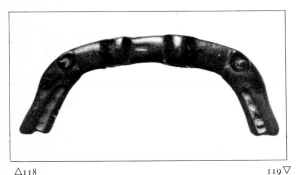

△118   119▽

118 Cheek-piece

Bronze; length 14.4cm.
Minusinsk Region. Chance find. Collection
of I. P. Tovostin, 1913.
Tagar culture; 6th century BC.
Hermitage. 3975/324.
Unpublished.

Cheek-piece with two perforations, its curved
ends shaped in the form of slightly flattened
wolves' heads. The heads are executed with
great skill and the elongated muzzles and open
jaws, in which can be seen two fangs and two
rows of sharp teeth, are striking in their realism.
The eyes and the small flattened ears with scrolls
at their bases are finely modelled.

119 Battle-axe

Bronze; length 15.8cm.
Barrow near Lake Podgornoe, Krasnoyarsk
Region. Excavations of S. A. Teploukhov, 1926.
Tagar culture; 7th–6th centuries BC.
Hermitage. 4580/11.
Bibliography: Gryaznov, 1969. no. 37.

On the butt of the battle-axe (or pole-axe) is
represented a standing, two-headed beast with a
massive, clumsy body and thick pillar-like legs.
It has a long muzzle widening towards the
mouth, a bulging forehead, small ears and the
eyes and nostrils are conveyed by round
openings. In its jaws are two rows of sharp
teeth. On the body, which is divided by a
vertical groove, are three round openings whose
purpose is not clear.
  The shape of the axe, with its spade-ended
blade, is uncharacteristic of the Khakass-
Minusinsk basin. The same is true of the
representation of the animal, itself an
unidentified species.

120 Belt plaque

Bronze; length 9cm; width 5.2cm.
Pavlovshchina Village, Krasnoyarsk Region.
Chance find. Collection of I. A. Lopatin,
nineteenth century.
Tagar culture; 6th–5th centuries BC.
Hermitage. 5531/1395.
Bibliography: Zavitukhina, 1973. fig. 6.

Figure of a tiger in relief. The predatory nature of the beast is expressed by characteristic details – the large, bowed head, snarling jaws with large prominent fangs and the powerful claws. The eye-socket and drop-shaped eye are realistically rendered, a ruff accentuates the line of the jaw and the ear is represented as a scroll. The long tail is broken off at the end. Two pins with oval heads on the reverse served to attach the plaque to a strap and the large opening in the region of the shoulder-blade was for the same purpose.

Few similar plaques have been found in the Khakass-Minusinsk steppes and their style is closer to the representations of tigers on objects from the Altai and Tuva.

121 Socketed axe
Bronze; length 9.6cm; width 6.3cm.
Environs of Minusinsk, Krasnoyarsk Region.
Chance find. Collection of V. V. Radlov, 1863.
Tagar culture; 7th–6th centuries BC.
Hermitage. 1123/51.
Bibliography: Artamonov, 1973. fig. 137.

▽120   121△

△122

123 ▽

Wedge-shaped socketed axe, rectangular in section, embellished by two lugs in the form of stylised birds' heads, the smaller opening forming the eye. Around the upper edge runs a strip of incised triangular ornaments. On both sides of the blade are identical impressed designs of feline predatory animals with slim-waisted bodies, head turned backwards, and open, fanged jaws. Their curved legs terminate in birds' talons. The shoulder and haunch are represented conventionally as rounded shapes and the tail is raised and curls in a spiral.

The design of the ornament and the figures of the animals were impressed on the model from which the mould was made.

122 Socketed axe
Bronze; length 5.9cm; width 6cm.
Sayanskaya Village, Krasnoyarsk Region. Chance find. Collection of I. A. Lopatin, end of the nineteenth century.
Tagar culture; 6th–5th centuries BC.
Hermitage. 5531/97.
Unpublished.

Socketed axe in the form of a chopping blade with a four-sided socket. The symmetrically placed lugs are cast in the form of schematically stylised birds' heads with long, curved beaks and perforations for eyes. Judging by its small size the axe was a decorative or cult object.

123 Ferrule
Bronze; length 7.6cm; width 3.6cm.
Korkino Village, Krasnoyarsk Region.
Chance find. Collection of I. A. Lopatin, nineteenth century.
Tagar culture; 7th–6th centuries BC.
Hermitage. 5531/200.
Bibliography: Radlov, 1894. pl. XIX, fig. 3A, B.

Oval ferrule with a six-sided head ending in a four-sided point. The ferrule is decorated with an impressed ornament; on one side is the figure of a fish and a series of V-shapes, one within the other; on the other side are two similar arrangements of V-shapes. Ferrules were placed on the lower ends of the handles of battle-axes and could be used as weapons.

124 **Arrow-heads**

Bronze; lengths from 3.2cm to 4.5cm.
Kamenka, burial ground 1, Krasnoyarsk Region.
Excavations of Ya. A. Sher, 1963.
Tagar culture; 7th century BC.
Hermitage. 2440/35.
Unpublished.

Fifty-seven of these bronze arrow-heads – the contents of a single quiver – were found in one grave. They fall into several types: two- and three-bladed, leaf-shaped with backward pointing barbs and bullet-shaped. All had sockets, either protruding or concealed. Examples of various types are exhibited.

125–127 **Arrow-heads**

Bone; lengths 9.5cm, 10.4cm, and 4.7cm.
Barrow near Lake Podgornoe, Krasnoyarsk Region. Excavations of S. A. Teploukhov, 1926.
Tagar culture; 7th–6th centuries BC.
Hermitage. 4580/65, 68, 83.
Unpublished.

Bone arrow-heads with shafts were widely used in Siberia. The bullet-shaped arrow-head with a socket is an imitation of a bronze original.

   These arrow-heads come from a single quiver, which contained ten arrow-heads of bone and eight of bronze, the latter similar to those in no. 124. Together with the fragments of the leather quiver they were found near the left forearm of the body of a warrior who was equipped also with a dagger, a battle-axe with a ferrule, a knife and other objects.

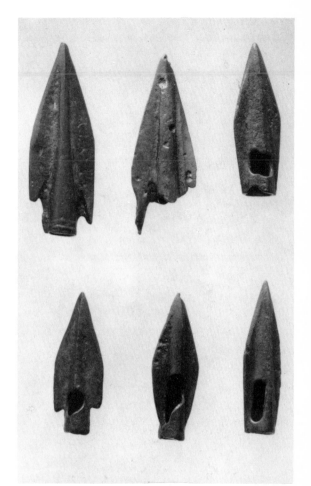

△124

125-7▽

THE TASHTYK CULTURE
Catalogue numbers 128–136

The final centuries before the birth of Christ saw great changes for the peoples of Central Asia, and the powerful tribal unions of the nomadic and warlike Huns, who entered the scene at this time and also influenced Southern Siberia.

In the first century BC a new culture can be recognised in the Minusinsk basin, along the river Tashtyk. Iron was now the most important metal, and both tools and weapons have been found in abundance. Like their precursors, the Tashtyk tribes practised agriculture as well as being semi-nomadic pasturalists. They used ploughs with iron plough-shares, as well as mattocks, sowed a variety of cereals, harvested grain with iron sickles, and then ground it on millstones. Among their animals, horses and sheep took pride of place. Hunting played a significant role and supplied the skins of deer, wild goat, wolf, sable and otter.

In 1969, in the Oglakhty mountains on the left bank of the Yenisei, Professor L. R. Kyzlasov at the head of the Khakass Archaeological Expedition of Moscow University excavated a tomb of the first century BC which had not been looted. A low wooden chamber, surrounded by layers of birch bark, had been kept hermetically sealed. The dry soil and steep slope of the ground had prevented moisture from entering, and so everything was perfectly preserved. In the tomb were the bodies of a man and a woman in full winter dress with coloured plaster masks on their faces. Alongside were two man-size leather dolls, stuffed with grass and dressed in the same winter clothing as the bodies. Inside each doll there was a pouch containing cremated human bones; it was evident therefore that the dolls represented cremated human beings, so one and the same tomb had a mixture of two quite different burial rites. Other discoveries in this tomb included wooden vessels (cat. nos. 129, 130), pots, leather and wooden pillows, miniature bridles with iron bits, and a fur quiver containing the shafts of arrows whose points had been removed. The plaster masks (cat. no. 136) and the clothing (cat. no. 128) are exceptionally important.

On the right bank of the Yenisei, near Mount Tepsei, in 1968 and 1970 Gryaznov excavated third century AD burial vaults of the Tashtyk culture. The wood-lined vaults had been set on fire; the absence of oxygen meant that the wooden objects had not been completely destroyed, only charred. Finds included figures of animals (cat. no. 133), ornamental vessels (cat. no. 134), and seven plaques with incised scenes of fighting animals (cat. no. 135).

128 Fur coat

Fur; length: back 35cm; front 43cm; sleeve 23cm.
Grave in the Oglakhty Mountains, Krasnoyarsk
Region. Excavations of L. R. Kyzlasov, 1969.
Tashtyk culture; 1st century BC.
Hermitage. KP-69 no. 2.
Unpublished.

Child's fur coat made of sheep-skin. The front is
edged with dog or wolf fur and trimmed with a
narrow strip of sable. The skirts are cut from a
single piece of sheep-skin and have gussets let
into the sides causing the coat to flare towards
the hem. The edges of the front are made up of
small pieces of dog fur and merge into a standing
collar. The arm consists of a shoulder portion
and a sleeve which was edged with a strip of
sable. For durability and in order to prevent the
penetration of water, a strip of leather folded
double was inserted in the seams of the shoulder
and the outer seams of the arms (which were
sewn up first). This is a technique also known
among the Pazyryk tribes. The coat is cut to
resemble adult garments but the front was not
intended to overlap, unlike adults' fur coats
which were held closed by small straps.

The coat was discovered in the Hermitage
during conservation. It had been placed – for
some unknown purpose – under the back of a
man's corpse (cat. no. 136) which was dressed in
two fur coats – one with the fur inside next to
the skin and one over the top with the fur
outside.

128

129 Dish
Wood; length 34cm; width 23.7cm.
Grave in the Oglakhty Mountains, Krasnoyarsk
Region. Excavations of L. R. Kyzlasov, 1969.
Tashtyk culture; 1st century BC.
Hermitage. KP-69 no. 10.
Bibliography: Kyzlasov, 1971. Abb. 2.

Oval, rimmed dish used for cutting and serving
meat. Such wooden plates and dishes were
widely used by the tribes of Southern Siberia in
the last years BC and the early years AD together
with moulded earthenware vessels. A transverse
crack in the dish is held together by a strap
threaded through holes bored in the rim (a
repair made in antiquity). The hole near the
edge was to hang the dish up when not in use.

130 Ladle
Wood; length 30.5cm.
Grave in the Oglakhty Mountains, Krasnoyarsk
Region. Excavations of L. R. Kyzlasov, 1969.
Tashtyk culture; 1st century BC.
Hermitage. KP-69 no. 9.
Bibliography: Kyzlasov, 1971. Abb. 2.

Ladle with a round bowl and a long handle,
carved from a single piece of wood. This
ladle was found in an earthenware vessel and used
as a serving
spoon.

131 Pin
Bone; length 12.8cm.
Grave near Novaya Chernaya Village,
Krasnoyarsk Region. Excavations of
E. B. Vadetskaya, 1967.
Tashtyk culture; 1st century BC.
Hermitage. 2573/26.
Bibliography: Dawn of Art, nos. 78, 79.

On the circular head of this pin, (a woman's
hair-decoration) is a delicately carved heraldic
composition of two miniature kneeling goats in
the round, their figures slightly flattened. The
goats' heads, which meet at the forehead, are
rendered as conventionally elongated ovals and
the horns, which curve down to meet the spine,
are embellished with transverse grooves and are
separated by a longitudinal furrow. Below the
head of the pin on the shaft are two
symmetrically-shaped lugs. The upper part of
the pin thus forms a unified, openwork,
decorative composition carved from a single
piece of bone.

129

130

132 Figurine of a wild ass
Bronze; length 3.3cm; height 3.5cm.
Minusinsk District, Krasnoyarsk Region.
Chance find. Collection of I. A. Lopatin,
nineteenth century.
Tashtyk culture; 1st century BC.
Hermitage. 5531/1402.
Bibliography. Kyzlasov, 1960. p. 92, fig. 33/3.

Hollow cast figure in the round of a reclining
wild ass. The small inclined head with
vertical elongated ears is set on a long
neck and the eyes, nostrils and mouth
are indicated by shallow pits. The
fore and hind legs are folded to form
a horizontal line, separated from the
body by a hollow space. The function of
the figure is unclear.
This pose is very reminiscent of the reclining
deer motif which is widely distributed in
Scytho-Siberian art.

133 Figure of a ram
Charred wood, gold; length 10cm; height 6.3cm.
Burial vault no. 2, Mt. Tepsey, Krasnoyarsk
Region. Excavations of M. P. Gryaznov, 1970.
Tashtyk culture; 3rd century AD.
Hermitage. 2616/151.
Bibliography: Ancient Siberia, p. 109.

This figure of a ram reclining with its legs
folded under it, the hooves together, produces a
monumental effect. Carved from a single piece
of wood the figure is highly stylised, only the
head, with its curving horns, and the hind
quarters (which are those of the fat-tailed breed
of sheep) being rendered in detail. The figure
was originally covered with gold-leaf.
Wooden sculptures of animals occur
frequently in Tashtyk art. Such
statuettes were probably placed in
graves as evidence for the large
numbers of domestic animals
possessed by the deceased. The
tradition of making such figures was
widespread in Southern Siberia
throughout the first millennium AD.

131

132

133

134

134 Vessel

Charred wood; width 14.7cm; height 15.2cm.
Burial vault no. 2, Mt. Tepsey, Krasnoyarsk
Region. Excavations of M. P. Gryaznov, 1970.
Tashtyk culture; 3rd century AD.
Hermitage. 2616/154.
Unpublished.

Cylindrical vessel, broadening towards the base,
carved from a single piece of wood. On either
side of the base are rectangular slots into which
are glued triangular legs. The front side of the
vessel is decorated with a chequered pattern in
which red-coloured squares alternate with
squares veneered with strips of match-wood.

The decoration on the bottom of the vessel
and on the lowest row of the reverse side is
simpler; here uncoloured squares alternate with
coloured squares hatched with incised lines.

135 Plank with designs

Charred wood; length 46cm; width 5.5cm.
Burial vault no. 1, Mt. Tepsey, Krasnoyarsk
Region. Excavations of M. P. Gryaznov, 1968.
Tashtyk culture; 3rd century AD.
Hermitage. 2616/30.
Bibliography: Gryaznov, 1971. p. 100, fig. 3/3, 4.

Thin wooden plank, decorated on both sides
with representations of men and animals. The
outlines were made with narrow, deep cuts,
but the hatching-lines are finer.

In the centre of the upper side is a horse with a
raised tail – a predatory animal with a spotted
skin perches on its crupper. To the left of the
horse a man, shielded by an ornamented man-
sized object, is pulling the horse towards himself.
On the left-hand portion of the plank is an
immense fleeing bear with large claws and to the
right of the centre are four human figures, the
first chasing the horse whilst the next, in mid-
leap, shoots an arrow. Behind him a warrior,
wounded by an arrow in the hip and with a bow
in his outstretched hand, runs to the right to
meet the last figure, of which only the upper
portion has been preserved. The warriors have
bows and arrows and rectangular quivers. The
designs narrate mythical or legendary events of
the period.

△135

135 details ▽

On the reverse are the usual representations of animals – four deer, their branching antlers extending along their backs, galloping headlong towards the right.

The ends of the plank have been lost. It was originally fitted with a handle.

136 Mask on the head of a man
Painted plaster; height 20cm.
Grave near Mt. Oglakhty, Krasnoyarsk Region.
Excavations of L. R. Kyzlasov, 1969.
Tashtyk culture; 1st century BC.
Hermitage. KP-69 no. 3.
Bibliography: Kovalenko, 1972. p. 78.

The mask covers the front portion of the man's head and through a rectangular hole on the crown protrudes long chestnut-coloured hair. Formed of a thin layer of plaster the mask was carefully modelled to preserve the likeness of the face, and is tinted red. On the red background there is a design in black paint: two stripes with pointed ends run from the right temple to the forehead and nose; another stripe runs to meet them from the left temple towards the eye where it divides into two forks, the lower of which has three barbs. This design probably imitates tattooing. The mask fits the head tightly on the crown and by the ear and cannot be removed. Before the plaster was applied the eyes and the mouth were covered with fragments of silk, and the corpse was trepanned to remove the brain through a hole made in the region of the left temple. On the head of the corpse was placed a fur hat with ear-flaps with a sable pelt sewn to the front, fur inside, in such a way as to cover the face of the mask.

X-ray examination of the skull has revealed European-type features. The portrait-mask also has an elongated European shape of face.

A woman's mask found in this grave was made in the same manner as the man's but differed from it in its colour, ornament, and the absence of an opening on the crown.
Colour plate

BIBLIOGRAPHY

SAI   *Svod arkheologicheskikh istochnikov*
(Collection of Archaeological Sources)

SGE   *Soobshcheniya Gosudarstvennogo Ermitazha*
(Reports of the State Hermitage)

ASGE   *Arkheologichesky sbornik Gosudarstvennogo Ermitazha*
(Archaeological Journal of the State Hermitage)

KSIA   *Kratkie soobshcheniya Instituta arkheologii
Akademii nauk SSSR*
(Brief Reports of the Institute of Archaeology
of the Academy of Sciences of the USSR)

Ancient Siberia   *Drevnyaya Sibir'. Putevoditel' po vystavke* (Ancient
Siberia. Exhibition Guide). Leningrad, 1976.

Artamonov, 1973   M. I. Artamonov. *Sokrovishcha Sakov* (Treasures of
the Sacae). Moscow, 1973.

Borovka, 1928   G. Borovka. *Scythian Art.* London 1928.

Dawn of Art   *The Dawn of Art. Drevnee iskusstvo.* Leningrad, 1974.

Devlet, 1969   M. A. Devlet. *Arkheologicheskoe izuchenie Yuzhnoy
Sibiri v gody sovetskoy vlasti* (Investigations into the
Archaeology of Southern Siberia in the Soviet
Period). KSIA, 118. Moscow, 1969.

Gryaznov, 1958   M. P. Gryaznov. *Drevnee iskusstvo Altaya* (The
Ancient Art of the Altai). Leningrad, 1958.

Gryaznov, 1969   *Southern Siberia.* London, 1969.

Gryaznov, 1971   M. P. Gryaznov. *Miniatyury Tashtykskoy kul'tury*
(Miniatures of Tashtyk Culture). ASGE, 13.
Leningrad, 1971.

Kovalenko, 1972   T. V. Kovalenko. *Restavratsiya gipsovykh pogrebal'nykh
masok* (The Conservation of Plaster Burial Masks).
SGE, 35. Leningrad, 1972.

Kyzlasov, 1960   L. R. Kyzlasov. *Tashtykskaya epokha v istorii
Khakassko – Minusinskoy kotloviny* (The Tashtyk
Epoch in the History of the Khakass-Minusinsk
Basin). Moscow University, 1960.

Kyzlasov, 1971   L. R. Kyzlasov. *Das Grabmal am Jenissej. Ideen des exakten Wissens*, 'Wissenschaft und Technik in der Sowjetunion' 8. Stuttgart, 1971.

Radlov, 1894   V. V. Radlov. *Sibirskie drevnosti* (Antiquities of Siberia), vol. 1, fasc. 3. St Petersburg, 1894.

Rudenko, 1960   S. I. Rudenko. *Kul'tura naseleniya Tsentral'nogo Altaya v skifskoe vrema* (The Culture of the Population of the Central Altai in the Scythian Period). Moscow, Leningrad, 1960

Rudenko, 1962   S. I. Rudenko. *Sibirskaya kollektsiya Petra I* (The Siberian Collection of Peter the Great). SAI, vyp. D319. Moscow, Leningrad, 1962.

Rudenko, 1966   *Die Sibirische Sammlung Peters I. Ubersetzung aus dem russischen von H. Pollems*. 2. Auflage. Berlin, 1966.

Rudenko, 1970   S. I. Rudenko. *The Frozen Tombs of Siberia*. London, 1970.

Scythian.. Art, 1969   *Scythian, Persian and Central Asian Art from the Hermitage Collection*. Leningrad, Tokyo Museum, 1969.

Unesco, 1976   'The Scythians'. *UNESCO Courier*, December, 1976.

Zavitukhina, 1973   M. P. Zavitukhina. *Tagarskaya kul'tura na Enisee. Kratky putevoditel'* (The Tagar Culture on the Yenisei. Short Guide). Leningrad, 1973.

Zavitukhina, 1978   M. P. Zavitukhina. *Kollektsiya G. F. Millera iz Sibiri – odno iz drevneyshikh arkheologicheskikh sobrany Rossii* (G. F. Miller's Siberian Collection – one of Russia's Oldest Archaeological Collections). SGE, vyp. 43. Leningrad, 1978.